HIDDEN IN THE HEART

A GLORIOUS SECRET

(ONE WOMAN'S JOURNEY TOWARD WHOLENESS)

BY NITA ANDERS

Cover design: Portrait of the author, by Laura Anders Shepard

First published by Dog Ear Publishing
4010 W. 86th Street, Ste H
Indianapolis, IN 46268
www.dogearpublishing.net

dog ear
PUBLISHING

ISBN: 978-160844-003-0

This book is printed on acid-free paper.

Printed in the United States of America

DEDICATION

To my daughter, Sally Katherine Anders, her children,
Jacob (Kristi) Cowham and their son, Finley; Ryan (Jackie)
Cowham and their children, Sydney, Dakota, Mark,
and Grace Elizabeth; and Thomas Cowham.

To my daughter, Laura Jean Shepard (Leonard), their children;
Sara, Ben (Emily) and their son, Robert; and Scott Shepard.

To my son, William Scott Anders (Mary Barrett) and their children;
Carolyn; Robert (Emily) and their sons, Wesley and Ryan;
and Mary (Patrick) Keating.

And to all who come after….

Acknowledgments

To friends who proofed the early copy, and to Louise Sample, for the final edit. To my daughter, Laura Shepard, for helpful comments and her portrait of me on the front cover.

To Professional Editors; Celese Rie, John Niendorff, and Barbara McNichols, for their guidance and direction along the way.

A special thanks to Dr. Ernest Holmes and Dr. Brugh Joy for their uniquely different teachings of Spirit and of Truth.

For the love and encouragement of my husband and children, and to those who've supported me in so many ways in getting this book into print; I am most grateful.

CONTENTS

PART II: BODY AND SOUL

"I said to the man who stood at the gate of the year,
Give me a light that I may tread safely into the unknown,
and he replied, "Go out into the darkness and put your hand
into the hand of God. That shall be to you better than light
and safer than a known way."
(From a plaque in St. George's Chapel - Windsor Castle)

PART III: SYNTHESIS INTO WHOLENESS

It is only with the heart that one can see rightly;
What is essential is invisible to the eye."
Antoine de Saint-Exupery

Prologue

This book is a testament to the awakening spirit; of how a spiritual epiphany became the catalyst for my inner transformation. My intention is not to promote any particular religion or philosophy as the right and only way to God, but to share how this new revelation changed my life's direction and purpose. I wish to 'shout from the rooftops' some general spiritual facts I now regard as central truths:

- **God is real—a living spiritual Presence and Power in the world here and now—waiting to be recognized and called into action against the forces of evil that seem at times to overwhelm us.**
- **When we become conscious of the nearness of God, our fears are abated and our faith restored.**
- **The kingdom of heaven is within—and we must go within to find it.**

The insights I share in this book have unfolded as a gradual process over many years. My path to discover more of God's truth quite naturally became a path of self-discovery as well. While we are uniquely individual in our *conscious* understanding and experience of God and in our own sense of self, I believe, at *unconscious* levels, we carry universal patterns common to the human species. Therefore, whether you are a seeker of Truth, a long-time believer, or a skeptic, I hope you will find elements of truth here that resonate with your soul. If, by chance, some of my experiences enhance your realization of God, or inspire and support you on your journey, I am grateful.

* * *

Some of the stress factors that may have contributed to the crisis that awakened me are briefly outlined here. The summer of 1972 our family moved from Southern California back to Tulsa, Oklahoma where we had lived in the mid-50's. Sally, our oldest, was now married and our daughter, Laura, was entering college that fall. Our son, Scott, would begin his senior year of high school in September.

Time was running out for me to find that elusive "something" that would fill my life with meaning once the children left home. Several years earlier I had begun my search, taking continuing education classes at a local community college. None had identified a strong career path; however, in one of my classes I was introduced to the book, *The Feminine Mystique*, by Betty Freidan. As we read and discussed the ideas presented—without warning, I discovered a hidden rage.

What a totally unexpected turn of events! Interestingly, this rage didn't erupt as a tantrum or angry assaults against the men in my life or, for that matter, against men in general. The men in my life were wonderful. I loved them and they loved me—my husband, son, father, father-in-law, and some favorite uncles. In general, all of my associations with men had been pleasant. Oddly, this rage seemed to extend beyond the personal. Freidan had not only touched a nerve in my psyche, but evidently in the psyche of millions of women who felt as I did—that our male-dominated society and religion have for centuries kept women from living true to their full potential.

* * *

Other stress factors were, first of all, the continuing deterioration of my young sister's health. Judy, diagnosed with lupus erythematosus in her early teens, had suffered frequent major and minor crises over a period of twelve years. Unable to be of physical support to her or my parents in Mississippi, I could only stay in touch and worry. In 1970 my beloved father-in-law died. That same year I lost a kidney due to flu complications. Six months later a pressure in my chest was diagnosed as menopausal. A hormone shot every six weeks readily solved this problem, and magically, I felt like a new person.

Back in Tulsa, assuming my former doctor would continue the hormone treatments begun in California, he flatly refused. In fact, he took me off hormones "cold turkey," convinced that hormone therapy had been a major factor in the cancer deaths of a number of close family members. Two or three weeks later I experienced an acute attack of rheumatoid arthritis in both hands. The suddenness of its onset and the accompanying pain caught me completely off-guard.

Rather than return to the doctor who had refused hormone treatment, I searched for another since, whether it was true or not, I associated the termination of hormones with this new and frightening turn of events. I hoped another physician would have a simple cure, but sadly, his diagnosis was "rheumatoid arthritis." The dictionary's description of this disease is "chronic and incurable, marked by stiffness and inflammation of the joints, weakness, loss of mobility, and deformity." Devastating news! In this case, all the doctor could do was help control the pain. At least I could be grateful for that. The stress of these earlier events were, no doubt, contributing factors, still I believe the abrupt curtailment of hormones was the trigger.

Note on divine gender

I do not believe God is a male figure, but rather an Infinite Spirit, and the spiritual embodiment of all we define as masculine and feminine. This view seems to contradict the perception of God as "Father" in most major religions. I believe that God is the "Creator of all that is," not only cosmic and universal, but also in you and me as a Holy Presence. Even so, out of familiarity, in this book I have chosen to use the personal term, "Father."

In the *New Testament*, Jesus personifies both the masculine and feminine aspects of God in the display of his powers, his compassion, and his unconditional love. Yet the writers of the *Bible*, reflecting their ancient, deeply patriarchal mind-set, failed to identify this feminine aspect, in him and in the Trinity. They failed, as many do today, to honor and appreciate both the masculine and feminine traits in God; in the man, Jesus; as well as in ourselves. Jesus defined God as "A Spirit, and we must worship him in spirit and in truth."

From *Genesis* – Chapter 1:26,27 …"And God said, Let *us* make man in *our* image, after *our* likeness….So God created man in his *own* image, in the image of God created he him, *male and female* created he them." (my italics.)

* All *Bible* references are from the *Authorized King James Version, Red Letter Edition.*

PART I:

M IND AND SPIRIT

Epigram:
"Ask, and it shall be given you,
Seek, and ye shall find,
Knock, and it shall be opened unto you."
Mark 7:7

Chapter 1

"Blessed are the poor in spirit;
for theirs is the kingdom of heaven."
Matt. 5:3

The "Beatitudes of Jesus" had always been a mystery to me, but this mystery was about to be solved. To say I was depressed and miserable that crisp, sunny September morning in 1972 would be a major understatement. How in heaven's name was I going to cope with this debilitating pain and come to terms with a progressive disease that had no cure? In a sort of stupor I watched two squirrels chase each other up and around the big elm tree on our front lawn—so full of life—yet I was unable to fully appreciate the scene. I could only think about my loss of energy and vitality—and more specifically my pain. Everything brought my thoughts back to the constant, throbbing pain in my hands.

The pain had intensified significantly since the doctor's recent diagnosis of rheumatoid arthritis. The knuckles across both hands were red, swollen, and hot with fever. (If fever was otherwise present in my body, I was not aware of it, I was only aware of the acute pain in my hands.) These past few weeks ordinary chores had become increasingly difficult and a few impossible to perform. The realization that this situation could get worse before it got better, IF it got better, had depleted my mental, emotional, and physical energies. My sole activity was spent counting the hours and minutes until I could again take medication. Try as I may, I could not get my mind off my pain and this tragic turn of events.

As I sat feeling very sorry for myself that particular morning, I heard a voice. Sitting alone, I knew in an instant that it didn't come from outside of me; rather it seemed to originate from somewhere within me, yet I knew "I" had not said anything. This inner voice simply said, "Pray." Given my religious upbringing, one would assume that personal, private prayer was a natural part of my life, but strangely it wasn't. I had heard hundreds of prayers in my lifetime, so the formula was familiar. I had also listened to and repeated prayers innumerable times. Yet when I actually thought about it, I couldn't remember ever having begun a prayer on my own.

After all my years spent in the church I had to wonder why this was so. Was it because I felt my life was working fine without the intercession of God? Maybe, but the answer could also have been my inability to conceive of God, the father; Christ Jesus, the son; and the Holy Spirit as close enough or real enough to hear and respond to my prayers. Now, confronted by this mysterious voice, my first priority, rather than follow instructions, was to understand what was actually taking place. I asked myself with surprising boldness: was this the voice of God? And if so, what exactly was I to pray for—a physical healing? I kept up this line of questioning, all the while resisting the command to pray. Was my hesitancy a need to understand or just willful stubbornness? I thought perhaps a bit of both.

Some minutes passed before the voice, stronger now, again said, "*Pray.*" At that point I was suddenly overcome with a deep sense of shame and humiliation. What was happening to me? Where were these feelings coming from? They seemed to be rising from somewhere deep within me as feelings I didn't recognize as mine. Greatly mystified by the emotions sweeping over me, I was even more mystified by my continued resistance to the voice I had heard and the instructions I had been given. Unbending still, I made no move to pray.

Then, *emphatically,* the voice issued its last command: "*Go to your bedroom, kneel, and pray.*" At this point I was totally overwhelmed by the intensity of my emotions, and completely baffled by what was taken place in me. Weeping now and struggling to my feet, through my tears—still questioning—still resisting—I haltingly walked toward my bedroom. As I stood beside my bed, *still not wanting to kneel*, the physical pain, compounded a hundredfold by the pain of these powerful emotions, was simply too much. Falling to my knees, I barely mumbled the words—"*God help me.*" Then came this shocking afterthought, shocking because in that moment I realized, for the first time, the uncertainty of my belief—"If there *is* a God!"

Suddenly, from somewhere directly above and behind me, a strange kind of radiant light appeared. Although I didn't see it with opened eyes, I felt its radiance enter the top of my head and begin its descent into my body—not only as a powerful, pulsating Light/Energy, but simultaneously, as warmth, gentleness, and love. As this powerful, loving Light/Energy washed over and through me—in wave after wave after wave—I was swept up in an ecstasy beyond anything I could ever have imagined.

I felt as though a powerful, loving Spirit was embracing me, firmly yet gently. Time stood still as this awesome power continued to pulsate and reverberate through me, echoing and re-echoing a harmonic resonance through every cell in my body. Actually, I have no idea how long this mystical experience lasted—perhaps no more than several minutes. Nonetheless, it was long enough to forever change my life.

When the Light/Energy finally subsided, I slowly rose and walked into my kitchen. Still shaken, I sat down at our little breakfast table to ponder what had just transpired. Basking in the new and wonderful feelings that continued to gently flow through me, I felt cleansed, purified, lifted, healed, and blessed. Taking stock, I was amazed and elated to note that the pain in my hands was gone, and so was my despair. Surprisingly, I heard myself speaking these words, aloud and with emphasis: "Wherever this Light takes me, I will follow. Whatever I have to give up to follow this Light, I will give up." The words had come out of my mouth without my having known I was about to speak.

Immediately I felt a great rush of fear at the implications of my words. What had I meant? What might I have to "give up"—my family, my friends, my religion, perhaps even my marriage? But the words I had spoken so fervently came from somewhere above and beyond any concern for human circumstances and events. Committed, I knew I could not take them back, nor did I want to. Soon thereafter, the realization came that, with this most amazing gift, I had been firmly set on a path of discovery.

* * *

Slowly coming out of that renovating experience I awakened to find myself in a fresh new world. Everything seemed miraculously bathed in an iridescent glow. People, animals, and even the landscape became visions of breathtaking beauty. Objects appeared to emit a shimmering light as though wrapped in a starry blanket of cosmic love. I called this state of mind "the afterglow" as it rested somewhere between ordinary, everyday reality and the high spiritual energy I had so recently experienced. In this intermediate zone of consciousness, I was evidently still open to the influence of this Light/Energy.

This "afterglow" state of mind lingered five or six weeks before gradually fading away. During this period I felt an amazing amount of love and compassion for everyone and everything. I recall glancing out my window the day after my experience and seeing a woman across the street waiting for a bus. I had no idea who she was, yet I wanted to reach out to her, embrace her, and tell her how much I loved her. With tears in my eyes and an ache in my heart, I knew I couldn't do that. She would have thought I was crazy. In the eyes of this world I was.

At a shopping mall soon afterward a young man approached me holding out a religious tract. Wearing sandals and beads, with long hair and bushy beard he was the perfect picture of what, at that time, we called a "Jesus freak" (a hippie who had found Jesus). At least, that was how I immediately judged him. Out of habit I thought, "Oh no, I don't want anything to do with this guy." But then he smiled a most engaging smile. Our eyes met and, in that brief moment, immense love was exchanged between us. Astonished by this unexpected development, I was spellbound by what seemed an instant spiritual connection that transcended any mere exchange of glances or superficial judgments.

A similar thing happened a week later when I drove past a garbage truck in our neighborhood. The driver was sitting high above my eye level yet somehow, for whatever reason, our eyes met and in that split second I felt a recognition of some sort—though I knew I had never seen this man before. Something extraordinarily strange was going on here—beyond the range of normal human contact. Being open to a more intimate aspect of my inner being—one that allowed me to catch brief glimpses into the similarly intimate nature of random strangers—was indeed a mystery.

Two more incidents of this kind occurred during this "afterglow" period, one with an infant and another with a young child—both strangers in passing. In general, I've always loved observing babies and small children, and my own babies in particular. They are so open, honest, and unselfconscious. Yet these encounters were different. In each instance, as we looked into each other's eyes, I saw in their silent gaze what seemed to me the depth and wisdom of an old soul. I almost felt I was seeing into the soul of the universe, though of course I had no idea what I was actually seeing. Once these illuminations faded, I found myself back in the physical/material world I had left—*but not before these numinous events had stamped themselves indelibly on my mind and heart.*

* * *

I had entered midlife without any deep understanding of spiritual truths—completely unconscious of God as an active Presence in the world. Neither, despite my religious background, had I any knowledge or experience in the art of meditation, contemplation, or prayer. Only a short while before, I was experiencing terrible pain and depression. Now, for no reason I understood, I felt healed and blessed by a transcendent experience of unconditional love and power. Suddenly, I realized there was nothing I needed more than to know God's love and power in my life. There was nothing I wanted more than to develop an intimate relationship with this Spirit that had showered me with so much love.

In 1984, twelve years after this experience, the memory of it came back one morning out of an especially wonderful meditation. In a deeply relaxed state of mind, the words suddenly appeared, ripe and ready to be written down. The poem captures the essence of that day—my sorely troubled thoughts and feelings, my pain and resistance, and finally my movement toward the Light. Except for a few minor changes, it remains here as I first received it.

Sorely Troubled

Within the temple of my heart
I sat down to weep, for I was
Sorely troubled. Through my
Tears I saw a candle burning;
A central, steady flame. It
Seemed an invitation, calling
Me closer, but I remained.

I just wanted to stay with my
Tears. And I did. And I was
Sorely troubled. Through my
Tears and anguish, again I saw
The flame. It now seemed more
Appealing with its warmth and
Pulsing light.

But I sat immobile, still clinging
To my hurts. I did not move,
I would not move, And I was
Sorely troubled. Again, the light
Was there, beckoning, stronger
Still. Come sit with me, no
Strings attached.

Take what you will from my
Warm glow, no need to
Give it back. And I sat resolute,
Stubborn if you will,
Wishing somehow the light
Would come to me.
And I was sorely troubled.

Suddenly I felt a chill, a dampness
In the air. Still hesitant, some part
Of me was moved to make a choice.
What choice was there really?
Where else was there to look
But to this tiny light?
And I was sorely troubled.

When I turned to face the light,
It suddenly disappeared,
And in it's place was
Nothing but The Light,
And more than Light, It was
Peace and Strength and Joy,
Encompassing, overwhelming.

In that surrender, an instant
Transformation from tiny
Candle flame to brilliant
Incandescent Light. In awe
and Wonder, never could I have
Imagined Life was joy itself;
And wholeness, perfect peace.

Now—my heart no longer a
Place for tears of sadness,
No longer cold and dark,
For the spark of light that I am
Found the Source of all Light—
The Great I AM.
Now I am no more sorely troubled.

Chapter 2

"Prove all things; hold fast that which is good."
I Thessalonians 5:21

Indeed, what elements had come together in my life to create such a powerful experience? Was there a critical build-up of mental and emotional stress from fretting so long and hard over life's large and small problems that finally caused this breakthrough? Most likely! There was definitely acute physical pain, but other souls have, no doubt, suffered more mental, emotional, and physical distress than I had. Had they received such a blessing? Although I was spiritually starved as well, many people who were likewise starving had not received this kind of blessing. (Or had they, and like me found no one to believe their story?)

What role had I personally played in a sudden and complete reversal of my mental, emotional, physical, and spiritual condition—from one of unbending resistance, depression, and excruciating pain in one moment to a transforming experience of unconditional love and joy in the next? From what depths had come this voice that kept prodding and pushing me into compliance? Ultimately I had to accept these deeper issues of life as beyond one's human capacity to know. Why certain things, whatever they are, happen to certain people, whoever they are—as well as the gift of grace, itself—all remain eternal mysteries, unanswerable, unfathomable.

When I sat down to contemplate this dramatic event, I wondered if I could have experienced such wonderful feelings of health and well being if this Light/Energy were not from a spiritual Source? Not being knowledgeable about such energy as this, I was curious. I knew, for instance, that the universe brims with energy—from the cosmic energy of stars and galaxies in outer space to natural energies in and on the earth—as well as man-made energies, such as radio and television transmissions and common household electricity.

To me, the comparison that made the most sense was something akin to electricity, but even so, I knew that what I'd felt was not any kind of electricity with which I was familiar. I knew the powerful and dangerous characteristics of electricity, whether man-made or from nature. For certain I had not, for instance, touched an electrical wire or been struck by lightning. Besides, I had never heard of lightning strikes producing spiritual ecstasy or physical healing!

Although this energy had entered the crown of my head and moved powerfully through my body, in no way did it feel threatening. If anything, it had been an energizing and healing force. No, this was some *other* kind of energy, different from anything I knew. To my knowledge this particular energy was undocumented by the scientific community. Whatever its Source, this Energy seemed to infuse every nerve, bone, muscle, and organ with its pulsing Light. In a matter of seconds, I felt vibrantly alive, as every cell and atom in my body was quickened into new life. Most amazing was the fact that while I had experienced the Light physically, this Energy was clearly beyond the physical.

The discovery that such a spiritual energy existed and that it had become known to me in such a profound way was incredulous! Most remarkable, this Light/Energy had a religious quality to it—except religious wasn't exactly the right word. Its quality was beyond the narrow exclusive, sectarianism of any one religion. Although this Light/Energy felt personal to me in terms of its unconditional love and total acceptance, I felt its nature was universal and cosmic. Indeed, the idea that such a phenomenon could happen to an ordinary person was not within the scope of my knowledge nor, as far as I knew, within the scope of most people's knowledge.

Sensing this Light/Energy as a gift of grace, I was finally moved to call It "Spirit," a word that best describes God. Again, as I pondered this whole sequence of events, I saw that nothing had happened to change anything that fateful morning until I surrendered in obedience to the command to kneel and pray. What seems now so simple a thing to do as obey was probably the hardest thing I'd ever done. The difficulty in finally *surrendering my human ego to a higher Power*, my personal will to a higher Will, was extraordinary. Some time later I concluded that the voice telling me to pray was probably not the voice of God, but perhaps the cry of my soul in search of God. After all, God doesn't force grace upon anyone.

* * *

Several months later I decided to take another more critical look at what had actually happened—before, during, and following that transcendent experience. I wanted to study more closely and remember more precisely all the events and circumstances—to reevaluate this material for anything I might have missed. At this point, I didn't need to prove to anyone whether this experience was some kind of mental or psychic phenomenon or whether it was truly spiritual. But I did need to prove to *myself* that it was what I thought it was. I knew what I'd felt—that the Energy that had embraced me so powerfully and lovingly must have come from a "higher dimension." So my inquiry wasn't about determining its spiritual authenticity as much as it was to anchor my thoughts and feelings in some kind of mental construct: to find adequate words (for which I had none) to describe such an numinous event.

* * *

In that simple act of surrender the windows of heaven had opened. So overjoyed was I to find that *Spirit was real and ever-present*—I wanted to immediately tell the world, but found myself unable to speak. I had no words to adequately describe such a miraculous event. Therefore, in the beginning I was unable to share this glorious secret with anyone. Later, however, I thought I should at least try to tell my husband what had happened to me. After all, the power of this experience had drastically altered my thinking and believing and given me a new truth, a new vision, and a new purpose in life. The person with whom I shared my life deserved to know what had caused the changes.

Explaining these events from beginning to end—from the inner voice telling me to pray, to the experience of the Light/Energy sweeping through me, to its transforming effect on my mind, body, and soul—concluding with the luminous effects of the "afterglow" in which I was still immersed—he listened carefully. When I finished, he gave no sign of having understood anything I had said. His usual response to unfamiliar ideas was to remain silent until he could think them through, to find an answer that made sense to him. I knew, with his engineer's mind, he was having a hard time trying to find some familiar frame of reference to such an extraordinary, nonlinear event. Even though he couldn't explain or understand what I was saying, he knew that something quite spectacular had affected me deeply. Noticing an immediate positive, healing effect on my mental, emotional, and physical well-being, he gave me what I most needed—his love and support. That was enough.

Never once did he suggest that what I'd experienced might not have been authentically spiritual, nor did he ever attempt to undermine my belief in its reality. Neither did he appear concerned about my sanity. At the same time, he expressed no personal curiosity or any desire to know more than I had told him. He just seemed happy that I was happy. I would have liked him to be more interested; yet he simply wasn't. Later I understood an elemental truth—that this spiritual experience was part of the awakening of my soul—not his. I soon found that his inability to make sense of an occurrence outside the range of what he regarded as normal or natural was not unique.

For events to make sense to us, they evidently must fall somewhere within the framework of our acquired ways of thinking and believing. Western society isn't inclined to accept anything that doesn't fit our rationally-based belief systems. This seems especially true for people like scientists and engineers who have been professionally trained to believe in the reality of Western rational thinking as the *only* reality, and that nothing else *can* possibly exist outside this reality. As a product of this culture, I thought that way myself before I had a direct experience of this spiritual Light/Energy.

My husband's reaction enabled me to see that sharing my story would present a challenge. Comprehending something so "otherworldly," especially from the outside looking in, would be too much of a stretch for the average person, sounding more like a fairy tale. Some might conclude "it was all in my head," that there was no real truth to it, or silently question my mental state. Nonetheless, I was desperate to talk to someone whose background might include historical or personal knowledge of spiritual epiphanies. Not knowing anyone outside my own Methodist religion, I naturally turned to our associate minister, who was also our pastoral counselor.

Psychologically trained to counsel parishioners, I hoped he would have some spiritual insight to share with me. With trepidation, but also with a joy I could scarcely contain, I recounted my story. He appeared to give me his solemn attention. When I finished, I sat quietly, expectantly waiting for his wise counsel. To my enormous shock and surprise, he had no questions or comments other than to say he didn't know what had actually happened to me but that I should keep a journal. That was the extent of the interview.

I felt his reaction would have been different if he had believed in the authenticity of my experience. Had he somehow come to an early conclusion that I was either high on drugs or had a mental problem? Was my story, in his mind, too bizarre, and my joy too great, to be the product of a balanced mind? I was deeply disappointed in his apparent lack of faith and belief in such a spiritual possibility. I had hoped he would have some understanding— or, at the least, show compassion and offer encouragement.

His cool dismissal of what I regarded as an authentic life-changing event was clearly a sign that *no one* was going to believe my story. At once I was overcome by a great sadness—if this man of the cloth couldn't relate, who could? I felt sad that neither he nor my husband had any inkling of what had happened to me. There was also sadness that there was simply no one to talk to, to celebrate with, or to share this marvelous truth. In that realization I felt *utterly* alone. I wondered how many others had experienced similar spiritual events without finding someone who could believe and understand?

Before finally giving up all attempts to share this event, months later I sought to confide in two old friends on separate occasions, only to be met with silence. I never knew precisely what they thought of my mental state or my story, though I could guess. The silence of friends brought renewed feelings of sadness and disappointment. The message was now clear—if I continued trying to tell my story, I would risk the possibility of ridicule and alienation.

From these silent and disbelieving reactions, I was suddenly aware of how much I needed and wanted the approval of others. More than anything else, I wanted *somebody* to believe in the reality of this renovating experience. However, I finally had to accept the fact that a "spiritual" experience that could not be validated by conventional scientific data was, at the very least, questionable—even among some clerics!

At this early stage of my development, I realized I simply didn't have the resources to convince anyone of the existence of a spiritual reality—here and now. I had learned the hard way that no one I knew was open to even consider such a radical idea of God responding to anyone in this manner. Thereafter, I avoided any mention of it in my conversations with friends and family, convinced they wouldn't understand. At the same time, my remembrance of that powerful, loving Light/Energy experience remained strong.

Gradually, I gained some perspective into how my husband, my pastoral counselor, and my friends may have perceived my story. It was simple, each had their traditional, individual beliefs about God. A modern-day spiritual epiphany simply didn't fit the framework of their belief system. Indeed, how could one be expected to believe such a phenomenon could occur—especially to ordinary people—unless, of course, that ordinary person happened to be you? In the final analysis, if an experience of this Light/Energy had happened to a family member or friend, I doubt I could have believed in its reality either—unless I had had a similar spiritual experience.

With the tepid reaction of my pastor, I felt traditional religion had again failed me. Much later, I was able to discern how this man probably felt when he heard my story. In his shoes, I might have come to the same conclusions. After all, his religious education was grounded not only in traditional Protestant theology but also in conventional psychology and its pathologies. As a counselor his training might have led him to believe more in the aberrations of the mind, and "ungodly" flights of imagination, than in the capacity of humans to experience the "transcendent." The probability that Spirit might profoundly touch a human being in the powerful, transforming way it had touched me was obviously beyond his knowledge and experience.

There are many deeply religious people who believe God no longer communicates with humanity except through a history written two thousand years ago. Based on my own experience I find this amazing. I absolutely do not discount the importance of Holy Scripture as a *foundation of truth and a major source of spiritual wisdom, guidance, and inspiration,* but that shouldn't discount the validity of contemporary spiritual experiences. I can understand why, to the devout, stories of encounters with God, or Spirit, by certain individuals in Biblical times would carry more weight and authority than similar experiences by ordinary people living today.

The Holy Scriptures contain a powerful mystique, providing us an opportunity to study eternal truths in the context of another time and place when God was believed to have walked and talked with humankind. Yet, the flip side to this belief is the implication that God is not an active presence in the world today. I doubt many people believe "God is alive and well right here and right now on planet earth." Possibly hundreds of thousands of souls have had a direct experience of a holy Presence and, like me, have been unable to find anyone to share this truth with. None so far have seemed able to hear the message that God, as a Living Spirit, is closer than our very breath.

Nonetheless, I felt strongly that this incredible experience was not just for my benefit only. I felt sure others could be healed and blessed from knowing the truth I had experienced—the truth that God, as Spirit, was/is a *real Presence and Power in the world today*—ready and waiting to respond to us the moment we turn and ask for what we need. But what did I know? What could I prove? With no obvious credibility or authority to speak for Truth, my task for now was simply to follow this "Light" wherever it might lead—gathering resources I would later need to communicate this truth.

Chapter 3

"And be not conformed to this world, but be ye transformed by the renewing of your mind, that ye may prove what is the good, and acceptable, and perfect will of God."
Romans 12:2

A quickening by this invisible Light/Energy had suddenly spread a whole new world before me—one of incredible love and beauty. The wonder of it had opened my mind and heart to know beyond all previous doubts the existence of a spiritual world—here and now. Not only had I felt a vibrant, healing Presence in, around, and through my being, I had also witnessed the after effects of this radiant Energy in a glowing landscape and in a select group of individuals. I personally felt this energy was from God; therefore I gave it the name "Spirit." Since it had responded to me the instant I turned to it I intuited that this Light/Energy must be present everywhere—in every living being.

More than anything I wanted to stay conscious of this spiritual Presence, but except for brief moments I could not. As mysteriously as this window to Spirit had opened—allowing me to glimpse another world, it had closed—leaving me with an acute sense of separation. (Was this feeling of separation the reason I had found it so hard to believe in the reality of God in the first place?) Seeking to reenter this Holy Space, on one occasion I found myself looking out onto a vast sweep of arctic plain—barren and empty. Another time a heavy, impenetrable curtain barred my way.

Were these images an indication of the enormous gap between my old beliefs and the new truth revealed? Before my experience in the Light I had not known what to believe. The idea of a *spiritual* dimension that could be accessed so powerfully while still in this physical dimension was not part of my belief system. Indeed, such an idea was beyond my wildest imaginings. Definitely, some of my beliefs were out of alignment with this amazing truth. If I wanted to cultivate an intimate relationship with Spirit—and I most certainly did—I could not revert back to my old ways of thinking and believing.

My aim was "to be transformed by the renewing of my mind"—to somehow bring my errant mind, my emotional fears, and my ailing body under the dominion of Spirit. If the thought had occurred to me to weigh and consider the cost of such an endeavor, of what obstacles I might have to face and overcome and what choices I might have to make along the way, I might have hesitated, but only for a moment. Without precedent this revelation of God as an ever-present reality had been so renovating to my soul, that I was totally committed.

In the days following my experience in the "Light" I thought of how the parable of the prodigal son, in a way, matched my own story. This familiar parable as told in Luke: 15:11-32, is a beautiful tale of a loving and forgiving father who is overcome with joy at the sight of his wayward son returning. He runs to meet him, gathering him in his arms, calling forth gifts to be bestowed upon him, and ordering a feast to be prepared in his honor. No recriminations, no accusations, no reprimands, no tears of sadness over what was done and past; only joy, compassion, forgiveness, and total unconditional love. "…Let us eat and be merry; For this my son was dead, and is alive again; he was lost, and is found."

I had felt this same sense of God's great love and forgiveness.

Much like the prodigal son, I may have known—unconsciously, if not consciously—that I had nowhere else to go and nowhere else to turn for help but to the Light of Spirit. Even as my conscious mind resisted, I may have recalled a hope or a dream from childhood—that maybe, just maybe, God was real and the prodigal son story was true.

I had always wanted to believe in the truth of this parable—that God was totally loving and forgiving—but the world I lived in didn't quite measure up. As far as I could tell, love always came with conditions. My observation was that one had to earn the love of family and friends, and of God as well. Therefore, this story and all the other beautiful promises in the *Bible* seemed more like fairy tales than reality—simply *too* good to be true.

The discovery that such a radiance of Light really did exist, within as well as without, unlocked the mystery of the ages for me. Now I understood that because God has given us free will, God must wait for us to discover the kingdom of heaven within ourselves. Jesus described this kingdom as "Neither, Lo here! or lo there! behold, the kingdom of God is within you." (Luke 17:21) Again in Matt. 13:44-46, he referred to the kingdom as "like unto" a treasure hidden in a field, and yet another time, as that pearl of great price. The metaphor that most perfectly described the kingdom for me was that of "buried treasure"—buried so deep within me I could not have guessed it had been there from the beginning.

* * *

In every culture, every nation, and every race—in Old World art and in all the world's scriptures there is evidence that God has touched and transformed human lives over the millennia. My knowledge of such people had come from the two-thousand-year-old documents of the *Old and New Testaments*. My first thought was that I was not, and would never be, in the same category as the mystics depicted in the *Holy Bible*. Yet, right behind that thought a kind of inner knowing came over me—that Spirit, still active in the world today, embraces the sinner as readily as the saint, the non-believer as easily as the believer, and the non-religious perhaps as often as the religious (or even the pseudo-religious, as I supposed I was before my experience in the Light.)

As I pondered these things, many questions came to mind. I recalled a verse from the Bible in which Jesus spoke of knowing a tree by its fruits. What had been the actual fruits of this experience? Was I better for it or worse? I examined my psyche to look for signs that I might have begun to lust for power or self-aggrandizement. I had not. Neither had I felt consumed by a desire to have my own way in the world or to control the lives of others. Nor had I felt moved to act unkindly toward others or to behave in a self-destructive way. In no way had I felt any hint of being taken over by dark, demonic forces.

What I *had* felt was the healing power of love and compassion, of gentleness and caring, of acceptance and forgiveness—and those feelings were far *stronger,* far *bigger,* far *wider* and far *deeper* than anything I'd ever felt before. This experience had not only imbued me with the power of its love but it had also left me with a great hunger and thirst for spiritual knowledge and understanding—and to again feel that oneness with Spirit. Suddenly I found myself "a seeker of truth"—eager to begin my journey toward independent thought, mature judgment, and positive action. Where this path would take me I didn't know but I knew I could rely on Spirit to guide me safely.

* * *

Wanting to find stories of ordinary people in modern times whose lives had been transformed by similar spiritual experiences, my search began in the library of the Methodist church. I found nothing there along those lines nor in Tulsa's main public library. Browsing through their supply of religious books I found no contemporary mystical experiences among them, yet the librarian might have directed me to the section on esoteric religious life had I thought to ask. The following day in the little branch library around the corner from my home I found the book I was looking for.

The title didn't suggest the mystical, spiritual experiences I thought I was looking for; nonetheless, this was the only book that caught and held my eye. The book was *The Science of Mind* by Dr. Ernest Holmes. I still marvel at how powerfully it drew and held my attention. When I opened it that evening, pieces of the spiritual puzzle I had tried to fit together all my life began to fall in place. In those early days, when my newness in Spirit was *so* new and the work of upgrading my belief system had only just begun, I didn't know Spirit was guiding me to a spiritual philosophy I had never heard of, but whose teachings would dovetail with my new-found awareness of Spirit as ever-present. Dr.Holmes' view of God was so much larger and more expansive than I had been exposed to in my early religious training.

In his book Dr. Holmes was describing God in ways I had not heard before—as Divine Mind, Infinite Spirit, Universal Intelligence—to name a few. Presenting universal truths that would require more study on my part, his use of modern language made these abstract principles much easier to grasp than the same truths found in the Bible. In an effort to better understand who we are in relationship to God, our Creator, Dr. Holmes spent many years studying both the Bible and human psychology. More specifically, he wanted to find practical ways to integrate Biblical truths into the fabric of our lives—for healing of mind, body, and spirit.

Although Jesus understood the inner workings of the human mind, this knowledge was unknown to civilization two thousand years ago. The study of human psychology is a fairly new science, and as such, knowledge of our own psychology is still unknown to the masses. The realization that our thoughts, feelings, and beliefs are continually weaving themselves into our life experiences, for good or ill, was a transforming discovery for me.

As an open-minded Christian with a scientific bent, Dr. Holmes' view of God as Divine Mind and Jesus as the epitome of a God-realized human being was very different from that of traditional Christians. He saw Jesus as a man who knew his kinship—not only with God as Father and Son, but with humanity as well. From contemplating how the Mind of God created the cosmos *on a grand scale* from his spoken word, Holmes deduced that in much the same manner God had given us the power to create *in miniature* our personal world from *our* thoughts, *our* beliefs, and *our* spoken word.

Holmes believed further that if our life experiences were unsatisfactory, we could un-create them and re-create them by changing the direction of our thoughts, the substance of our beliefs, and the power of our spoken word—from destructive and debilitating to constructive and healthy. This was up-dated language for the Biblical word—"repent." Repentence was not a common word in our everyday language and not as easy for me to grasp as just saying, "turn around and change directions."

Holmes believed that Jesus realized the divine potential within himself and based his life and teachings on the divine potential inherent in humanity. Holmes believed, as all Christians do, that Jesus was the example we were to follow—that he came to show us "*the way, the truth, and the light.*" His book, *The Science of Mind,* focused on the concept that our minds are intrinsically connected to the One Mind of God at subconscious levels—an idea completely new to me. I had thought of my own mind as being not only personal and individual but also separate and apart from God. Holmes believed that God was not only the Creator of all life from the beginning, but continues to be an infinite Source of love, wisdom, and creative power in the world today. His belief, that we are created in the image of God and do indeed "live and move and have our being in God," gave him a new truth affirmation that "there is One Life, that Life is God, and that Life is my life now." *

My interest began to peak as I read further. I wondered if there might be a local group of people studying this philosophy. Looking through the Yellow Pages, I found a Science of Mind Center** listed. The address was on the other side of town. At the time I was teaching a Sunday school class of teenagers at our Methodist Church. After class the following Sunday I decided to visit this Center. The format of the service was a bit unusual but from that first lecture I was drawn to this teaching as a starving person is drawn to life-giving food and water. I have no specific recollection of what the minister, Dr. Jean Amos, said that day but she gave life to Dr. Holmes' concept of God as Infinite Being, explaining further his ideas of the all-encompassing oneness, wholeness, and fullness of Spirit.

Every Sunday thereafter, following my class, I hurried across town barely in time to catch the eleven o'clock lecture. I kept this difficult schedule for almost two months, not wanting to abandon my class before it was scheduled to end. I had created the curriculum based on the Ten Commandments and their application in our lives today and had named it "What's so great about the *Bible*?" I not only had a personal interest in these lessons but in these young people as well. I felt they, and I, were learning a great deal—not just about spiritual truths, but also about ethics and Bible history.

I had thoroughly enjoyed creating this course, yet I now felt myself being pulled away. That's when I heard "the voice" again. I was on the freeway at the time hurrying across town to a Science of Mind service. I hadn't heard the voice—or anything like it—since that first encounter months before when I was told to pray. This time

* Science of Mind, page 292

** Footnote: This Science of Mind Center was also known as The United Church of Religious Science, affiliated with the corporate body based in Los Angeles, California.

the voice was so loud in my mind that, for a moment I felt sure it had come from some amplified outside source. The voice had that kind of impact.

What I heard was, "When the blind lead the blind, they both fall in the ditch." This time I was not caught up in the phenomenon of hearing a voice inside my head so much as I was astonished by the message. I remembered this *Bible* verse from childhood as a statement Jesus had made to his disciples (Matt. 15: 14). I had honestly thought I was teaching these young people valuable lessons in truth—*certainly not that I was blindly leading the blind.* I could hardly believe these words were meant for me—yet they obviously were. Coming from the Biblical Jesus I felt this was not so much a personal rebuke as it was a statement of truth I needed to hear.

The more I thought about these words and the way they had come to me the more I realized there were further implications. This statement was not just about teaching a Sunday school class of teenagers from my limited understanding of the *Bible.* For months I had been juggling my schedule—wanting to hold on to the old while also venturing out to test the new. Indeed, what I had been presenting as truth to those young teens may have been distorted by my balancing act—trying to be in two places at once, literally and figuratively. Badly shaken by this revelation, I became aware of another aspect of my blindness. I had been giving my time, energy, and money to one church and all the while being spiritually fed by another.

The statement, "When the blind lead the blind, they both fall in the ditch" wrapped up the issue succinctly—pointing out my "blindness" in assuming the role of a teacher of truth without any real spiritual understanding. Undoubtedly the time had come for me to seek after and find that greater understanding. Even though I hadn't consciously asked, "What shall I do—where shall I go in search of truth?" that had been my unspoken prayer for some time. The answer, for whatever reason, was not available to my conscious mind. The answer finally came from my subconscious storehouse of Biblical teachings.

Had that meaningful phrase spoken by Jesus not come into my awareness, I'm not sure I could have walked away from the "old" as cleanly as I did. Yet I believe this was the only answer that could have shocked me into positive action—to actually break away from the known and step out into the unknown. Through these words, I knew unequivocally that I was being directed by a higher source—by someone I could trust. Yet even with this sure directive I felt an ambivalence that was hard to shake—wanting to go and wanting to stay at the same time.

The churches I had grown up in felt so familiar, so comfortable—even if less than satisfactory. The people there were "my kind of people," and I understood that to walk away was to lose my old way of life. Yet after so many years of trying to live a traditional Christian lifestyle without gaining the spiritual understanding I'd longed for, nothing was left for me to do. The time had come for me to leave but I still couldn't believe I was *actually* leaving my traditional spiritual home. That was my first hurdle—the first thing I had to give up to follow the Light—and it was one of the hardest things I'd ever done.

That day I remember saying, "Wherever this Light takes me I will follow…." but then my next thought was, "What will mother and daddy think?" An astonishing question for a fifty year old to ask herself, yet that was my greatest concern! And what about friends and other family members? What would their reactions be? What if, by leaving the church, I ended up losing their love and approval? These thoughts revealed just how needy I felt in making this psycho-spiritual break with my past.

Fortunately I was able to *observe* these fearful thoughts without being consumed by them. Still I felt like a little child stepping out into a great void.

Oddly enough, I wasn't worried about my husband's or my children's responses. I knew somehow that even if they didn't always know what was going on with me, they would remain loving and supportive. Noting that my family and friends appeared happy and content in their faith I understood that their spiritual needs were being met in the traditional church. Would they wonder why I felt my needs *weren't* being met? Some part of me wondered the same thing.

I thought of two close friends I've known since grade school in the little Mississippi town of Prentiss. They have remained special friends—Bobbie and Ingram Foster—and are still active in the same Baptist Church we grew up in so long ago. Apparently they didn't have the questions I had as a young person about God. Rich in faith, these beautiful people have remained steadfast and loyal to their church all these years. On our travels south we note their continued dedication to serving God and humanity through their church.

My question remained—how were they able to comprehend the Bible teachings I had found so confusing—not only in my youth, but also in my adult life? Had they, and others with similar backgrounds, not had to struggle to find and develop a working relationship with God? Perhaps they had but were able to come to terms with their beliefs without having to leave their church. I have known many good people through my church affiliation—some of them the most loving, giving, and caring people one could meet. The characteristics common to each, besides their belief in God and Jesus, were a kind and generous heart.

On a few occasions I had observed in certain individuals another quality of spirit that was marvelous to behold. This quality was far more subtle and powerful than simple kindness or generosity. Through eye contact, a gentle touch, a warm smile, or a sincere handshake these people seemed to quietly and unobtrusively emanate an extraordinary radiance of love. Certain that I was witnessing God's love in expression, I wondered how these beautiful souls had come upon such a gift. Was this a reflection of their intimate relationship with the divine—a natural expression of their spiritual development? Were they born with this gift or was it something they had chosen to cultivate within themselves? Was it possible to attain such a quality in myself?

I confess I was not without envy as I watched and admired this amazing display of love coming from these individuals. I had grown up thinking that these traits of loving kindness and generosity, as well as this incredible radiance of love and light I was witnessing, were somehow exclusively "Christian." In later years I have seen these same qualities in people of other faiths and cultures, and realized that God's love doesn't always come dressed in traditional Christian garb. No matter how much we try to place God in a box of our personal and particular beliefs, this Universal God cannot be confined to human understanding. Simply stated, wherever love is, God is.

* * *

As I began the work of renewing my mind I remembered a verse from the *Bible* where Jesus reminded his disciples "to be *in* this world but not *of* it." Personally, I was very much caught up in *this* material world of lack and limitation—caught also in my fears of perhaps some day becoming physically deformed from the ravages of rheumatoid arthritis. How wonderful it would be if I could extricate myself from such a crippling belief. Pondering what this phrase meant I came up with an interpretation that we are wise to live in this visible, physical world without getting caught up in the circumstances of daily life, *as if it were the only reality.*

* * *

Wanting to steep myself in those qualities I equated with God—love, truth, beauty, I decided to give up reading the newspapers and watching television news programs as a first step. Until I could disaccociate myself emotionally from the disturbing stories of crime and violence, I felt this daily activity must be sacrificed. At the same time I carefully considered what television shows, plays, and films were worth viewing. Thus were my beginning attempts to focus on the positive in order to walk that invisible line between these two realities—the physical and the spiritual. Was it possible to reach a place in consciousness where I could be in this physical world with all its seeming limitations, and at the same time, be removed mentally, emotionally, and spiritually from the reality of it—to live in both worlds simultaneously?" My intention was to at least try.

When my teaching assignment was complete, I walked away from the old—consciously and freely, and with joyous anticipation—into the new. Never mind that the Methodist church was where we had raised our children and I had given many years in service. I understood that exchanging my familiar and comfortable traditional church environment for an unfamiliar and perhaps uncomfortable new teaching might present many challenges; nonetheless, I knew this was what I was supposed to do.

Chapter 4

"Judge not according to the appearance,
but judge righteous judgment."
John 7:24

Immediately I encountered major differences in this new church setting. The format for Sunday services was quite different from anything I had previously known. For the most part I welcomed the changes. First of all, the minister, Dr. Jean Amos, didn't sound like any preacher I had ever heard. The ministers I had known had a certain way of sermonizing and "preaching" that apparently came from their seminary training. She obviously was not trained in a traditional Christian theological seminary, but from a comprehensive study in the principles of the Science of Mind, from the best of Dr. Holmes's contemporaries. The clarity with which she outlined and elaborated the concepts of Science of Mind resonated with the truth I felt in my heart. Every week her message seemed not only meaningful for me, but also applicable to me. Likewise, I loved the prayer/meditations because they were affirmations of truth rather than supplications.

A major difference I observed on that first visit was a table in the foyer prominently displaying a prayer box and prayer-request forms for those seeking spiritual support for themselves or a loved one. Although the churches I had known believed in the power of prayer I had never seen an open invitation to write out a prayer request in any church I had ever attended. Also on the table was material relating to The Ministry of Prayer, known as the healing arm of the church, and a brochure introducing licensed Religious Science practitioners available by appointment for private prayer/counseling sessions. I was not familiar with the term "practitioner" and wondered who these people were. This was my introduction to the significant role of prayer in the study and practice of this philosophy, and I was duly impressed.

This Science of Mind Center didn't follow traditional convention in the format of their Sunday services, or in the functions and programs of the church. Besides an active Ministry of Prayer and licensed practitioners, there were also evening classes in the Science of Mind philosophy, as well as a bookstore with a large selection of inspirational and metaphysical books for sale after Sunday services. Spiritually hungry, I began a collection of books on spiritually-related subjects, garnering bits and pieces of truth from each one. Surprisingly, none of what I was reading contradicted what I held to be basic Biblical truths; in fact, they supported, amplified, and transmuted those truths into something more workable and practical for me.

Those few differences not to my liking became important lessons in awakening me to aspects of my nature I had, heretofore, not seen. The first lesson revealed my lifelong habit of judging by appearances. A bit disconcerting for me was the music—tending to be contemporary and celebratory rather than familiar and worshipful. I really missed the old hymns I had sung in my youth. Also different were the people drawn to this Center. Unlike the friends and neighbors I knew so well in my former church, the people who made up this congregation were not a homogeneous group. They came from miles around, from all walks of life, and from all rungs of the socioeconomic ladder. At first glance, none of us seemed to have much in common, but later, with opportunities to chat at the coffee hour and fellowship dinners—we found much to talk about. Like me, these people were also seekers of truth—on their own spiritual journeys.

A big bone of contention for me was the condition of the church building. Originally a synagogue, designated as an historic site by the city, it was badly in need of repairs. I was aghast at the plaster falling from the ceiling and the huge cracks in the steps leading up to the sanctuary. The kitchen and restroom facilities, though clean, hadn't been remodeled in at least twenty years. Why, I wondered, was a church that expounded the teaching of God's abundance unable to manifest prosperity in the form of a well-kept, attractive facility? Obviously, this membership didn't have the resources to fix the basics, much less restore this facility to its original condition.

This state of affairs bothered me more than I like to admit. I was judging and comparing this old building with the church buildings I was used to—those that were kept in mint condition by large and prosperous memberships. Suddenly I was aware of this tendency to judge and compare from appearances. Surprised and shocked by my strong negative reaction to the physical state of this building and to a membership that would allow such a state of disrepair, I had hoped my experience in the Light of Spirit had healed and elevated my mind to see beyond appearances. I was finding out otherwise. Whatever their origin, I noted the effects of my unkind judgments were affecting my sense of well being.

Looking at my early judgments of this situation years later, I realized this building was much too large an upkeep for our relatively small membership. Although there were enough dedicated members to financially support a smaller facility with ease, there were not enough to fund the restoration of this large decaying structure. At present they could only handle routine maintenance. Perhaps the minister and administrative board decided to keep this unwieldy piece of real estate, envisioning its ultimate resurrection through a growing membership—yet the building's run-down condition may have adversely affected that growth.

Nonetheless, in spite of these first few negative reactions and judgments, I found by far more good than bad. After all, Dr. Holmes's book. *The Science of Mind,* had brought me here and what kept me coming back was the way this teaching totally supported my newly awakened spirit. Here was a teaching that explains not only how the creative mind and nature of God works but also how the mind works to create life's experiences. Along with my beginning study of this philosophy, my desire to know more about spiritual truths, and my own psychology led me to voracious reading of books on these subjects. Unfortunately, each book was read without carefully noting author, title, or insights gained. My apologies to those many authors who added so much to my present understanding. If I had known at the time that I would someday write a book and need a reference file, I would have been more diligent.

I made some amazing discoveries in my readings—one of which was how we, as individuals, view our world. I had not really given much thought to how I perceived reality, or on what grounds I judged the personal lives of others. I was reminded that our perceptions of what we believe to be true, and our judgments about that truth, originate within our own mind. It *may* or *may not* be the truth of that person, place or thing. From our limited knowledge and understanding, we cannot know all the facts; therefore, our judgments may have little, or nothing, to do with the reality of the person or situation. "What is so" is personal and individual—formed not only out of the uniqueness of our personality and life experiences—but also influenced by our family, education, religion, and cultural environment.

As I mulled over this new information I couldn't deny that my perception of reality had some holes in it. Yet, I was beginning to see more clearly my formerly hidden judgments and prejudices for what they were. I wished this new awareness had been enough in itself to cause an instant turnaround in my habitual way of judging—but it wasn't as simple as that. While an insight into a new truth can happen in an instant, embodying that truth and turning it into a healthy, positive, and lasting habit is not instantaneous. After all, our thought patterns take years to develop. Replacing them with new patterns requires time and effort.

Initially I didn't approach this activity from a spiritual perspective, but rather from a psychological one. In this early developmental stage, I felt that asking God for help in this endeavor was somehow inappropriate. I felt I should be able to do this myself. Yet I did feel it appropriate to ask God for help in matters that were beyond my ability to handle. Once I realized I could not make these psychological changes on my own, I specifically asked God to heal my mind and spirit to facilitate the required changes. This marked the beginning of my understanding that I could ask God for anything!

My desire to develop a close relationship with Spirit was strong, but there was so much to learn I wondered if I was up to the task? I must change thoughts, attitudes, and beliefs that no longer rang true, and also learn true discernment, which was to judge, not from appearances, but from an inner sense of what was the right and good thing to do. For guidance in this area I had to listen for what has often been described as "that still small voice." Unfortunately, I was never told about this intuitive aspect of my nature; therefore, in the past whenever "that still small voice" came into my awareness I paid little heed. Unawares, I had absolutely no idea growing up that I could trust this quiet inner voice. Yet, this was my link to Spirit and the avenue through which deeper wisdom comes when I listen and heed its murmurings.

Overcoming this habit of making negative judgments meant I had to stay alert to my thought processes around judgment. My investigation was not to be pursued outside myself, but within myself—by observing the circumstances under which I usually became judgmental. Recognizing the need to change the ratio of negative and positive tendencies within my mind and heart, I began to concentrate altogether on the positive. Speaking positive truth affirmations outlined in my *Science of Mind* book, I began to reverse slowly the negative thoughts and feelings I had allowed to take root in my mind. My intention was not just to monitor these judgmental tendencies—but more importantly—to lift them up to the healing Light of Spirit.

As I began paying attention to my interactions with people, I made two important discoveries. My first insight was that with certain issues and/or certain individuals, my judgments could be decidedly strong. With others, I wasn't judgmental at all. Indeed, there was a marked difference between the way I reacted when I was emotionally involved and when I was not. The second insight was that in some gatherings, especially if I found myself differing with another person's viewpoint, instead of expressing my view, I would keep my opinions to myself, unknowingly allowing them to fester inside me.

Why did I keep silent and project an image of "nice?" Was it fear that if others knew my inner thoughts and feelings they might not like me? Absolutely! However, by not openly and honestly expressing my thoughts, feelings, ideas, and opinions with others, they began expressing as my inner critic. The old adage "if you can't say something nice, don't say anything at all" wouldn't have had a healing effect in my case. "Not saying anything at all" had actually been a convenient cover for my negative judgments. By projecting an outward appearance of "nice" I had kept hidden—even from myself—what was not so nice.

I set out to prove that through a systematic change in the direction and focus of my thinking, negative habits could in time be transformed. My developing strategy was to catch myself in the middle of making a critical judgment, then consciously turn it into a positive statement. For instance, if I caught myself critically judging what I thought was someone's faulty decision-making, I would immediately counter that thought with a reminder that, right or wrong, I was basing my opinion solely on external evidence. Why not have more empathy for that person? Using this procedure I rephrased those judgments in a truer, kinder light. Although I worked on mentally changing my thinking, I relied on prayer and the help of Spirit to attain true discernment.

Slowly—and not always steadily—reversals in my judgmental nature became noticeable. After three or four months of serious work, I realized one day that some things that had always "pushed my buttons' hardly upset me anymore. This new regimen for finding and healing critical judgments through positive affirmations seemed to be working! A bumper sticker from the 80's that read, "Look for the good and praise it," is a powerful affirmation and still one of my favorites. As I continue these practices I hope to develop ever greater sensitivity and compassion for others.

* * *

Another idea that came from extra-curriculum reading was the theory that our positive or negative reactions to others are aspects of ourselves that are otherwise hidden from our conscious awareness. For example, in the company of people I dislike or who upset me, I find their attitudes are a reflection of something in my own nature that I fear or don't want to know about. Likewise, in the company of those I most admire, my admiration is a reflection of aspects in my own nature I may not be able to see and claim for myself. Nonetheless, I questioned whether the attributes, good and bad, I saw in others were really unknown aspects of my own inherent potential. While I couldn't yet see a connection between my inner judge and the person I was judging, I felt that, in some mysterious way, we are connected to one another beyond our conscious knowing. From that viewpoint I could accept this idea as perhaps valid.

* * *

One Sunday morning, shortly after I had made my decision to join this new community of souls, a gentleman I had not seen before entered the sanctuary and sat down in front of me. Based on his outer appearance I made a quick judgment of him, and my immediate reaction was one of pity. He was middle-aged, clean-shaven, with carefully groomed hair, but dressed in an odd assortment of ill-fitting clothes. Who was he? He seemed to fit the description of a homeless person —someone with few resources, financial or otherwise. While those judgments might have been true, they might just as well have been false.

The following Sunday he joined our morning discussion group and shared these thoughts with us. He said, "We cannot know how far some of us have risen nor can we know how far many of us have traveled to arrive where we are today." Although I didn't know what circumstances he might be referring to in his own life, those words have stayed with me as a reminder never to judge a person by their outer appearance. My first judgments may have been correct—he might have been a recovering alcoholic or a transient on the move—however, the connotation of that view was completely misleading. Over the next few months, my impression of this man changed drastically as we chatted during coffee breaks.

He shared several of his poems with me. As I read them I sensed the depth of his understanding of the human spirit. Beneath what I had first judged "impoverished," was a man immensely rich in his inner life. From my encounter with this man I learned a valuable lesson about making superficial judgments. One cannot rightly judge people solely from outward appearances. He came and went, I know not where—but I remember him gently for the insights he gave me—and for the rare opportunity to see the common thread that binds us together as a human family!

As I became more conscious, I gradually gained new insights into a number of issues. For instance, my unhappy feelings about the poor condition of my church changed dramatically when my perceptions shifted from external conditions to deeper intrinsic values. I saw that the immediate work of our Science of Mind Center was not restoring this old building, but ministering to the needs of those who came seeking truth. What was needed was a place to study and worship, individually and collectively, in an atmosphere of openness, acceptance, and respect—a space in which people from all walks of life could explore new concepts of this thing we call God—to perhaps find a philosophy that more closely resonated with their deepest spiritual longings. Certainly that was why I was here.

* * *

In my encounter with the possibly homeless man, I realized that coming together in a common arena for a common purpose helps bridge the gap between strangers. I learned a valuable lesson, not to judge another from appearances only, especially those who seem so different from ourselves. I now understood a little better the meaning of Jesus' statement, "judge not the appearance," but I wanted to explore further the meaning of "judging righteous judgment."

Jesus' statement in Scripture was made to the Jews who admonished him for healing a man on the Sabbath. He understood that these men were searching for ways to incriminate him; therefore, their motives were unrighteous. When he used the term, "judging righteous judgment," he was evidently talking about the the ability to judge from a higher standard of intrinsic moral values and spiritual truths that transcend one's personal agenda.

Wanting to see and judge all things from a place of unconditional love and compassion, I knew full well that these qualities could not be accessed from my ego-centered sense of self. Unconditional love and deep compassion could only come through continued study of truth and from prayer and meditation—invoking Spirit to fill my heart and soul with the very presence of Love Itself. And so I found other references to judgments in the Bible. One was "Judge not, that ye be not judged. For with what judgment ye judge, ye shall be judged: and with what measure ye mete, it shall be measured to you again." (Matt. 7: 1) Another Bible verse that seemed to have a similar message was: "…whatsoever a man/woman soweth, that shall he/she also reap." (Gal. 6:7)

Studying these verses I saw with greater clarity how our judgments return to us the same kind of energy (good or bad) that we send forth. I began to understand how deeply we are subject to a universal, reciprocal law that *automatically brings back to us* that which *goes out from us*. Of that law, I had been ignorant. However, ignorance is no excuse, and no one is exempt.

These particular Bible references concerning judgments were not only excellent *general* principles worthy of my consideration but, more importantly, I now saw them as *specific* and valuable lessons I needed to put in place. Questions continued to come to mind around the issue of judging. I questioned whether there was a hidden agenda or underlying motive in my judging? Were my critical judgments of others a feeble attempt to feel better about myself? Was love to be found anywhere in my judgments?

Many insights came out of these periods of introspection, but the one that came as a complete surprise was to discover my own prejudice. This subtle oversight had conveniently escaped my notice before—that I held a prejudice against those I judged as prejudiced! Still, my most valuable lesson about judgments has come from the following Bible verse: "Why beholdest thou the mote that is in thy brother's/sister's eye, but considereth not the beam that is in thine own eye? Or how wilt thou say to thy brother/sister, Let me pull out the mote out of thine eye; and behold, a beam is in thine own eye? Thou hypocrite, first cast out the beam out of thine own eye; and then shall thou see clearly to cast out the mote out of thy brother's/sister's eye." (Matt. 7:3,4,5)

This statement has been a guiding principle in my continuing spiritual practice. During my years in the Science of Mind, even after I became a licensed practitioner and was serving others through the Ministry of Prayer and private practice, some part of me would occasionally ask why I didn't devote *less* time to the work of healing my own mind and heart and more time to serving others. When I questioned whether this was the true voice of Spirit, or some earlier orientation, this Bible verse about the mote and the beam would came to mind. I took this as divine counsel to continue my work of inner transformation. I have no doubt that Spirit, particularly in the form of this Bible verse, has helped keep me honest and spiritually on track, for I have been brought back—again and again—to the need to first take care of the beam in my own eye.

Chapter 5

"No man putteth a piece of new cloth unto an old garment… Neither do men put new wine into old bottles: else the bottles break, and the wine runneth out, and the bottles perish: but they put new wine into new bottles, and both are preserved."
Matt. 9:16,17

To counter my tendency toward negative thinking, I began using positive affirmations daily. Soon thereafter, I found myself submerged in a sea of negativity, my consciousness flooded with a multitude of fears, doubts, and suspicions. Inside my head a cacophony of voices were echoing what I had evidently assimilated in my youth as the "gospel" truth. Since not a single voice spoke in defense of these new ideas, I realized I had met the enemy and (like Pogo in the comic strip) found "the enemy was 'us'!" Puzzled as to what had triggered such a response I recalled this Bible verse about "new wine in old bottles." The metaphor here was that a new understanding of truth, like new wine, does not mix with old established beliefs.

Unwittingly, I had been working *overtime* to reprogram my deeper mind—never dreaming the practice of speaking affirmations could cause dissent, or anything other than immediate benefits. I had little knowledge of the contradictory nature of the unconscious mind, nor its range, depth, or emotional power. My new truths were still fragile and not fully grounded, which meant that my old beliefs were still very much in charge of my psyche. The 'old guard' must have realized how dangerous these daily affirmations were to the status quo. With all the power cards at their disposal they were fighting for their very existence. This experience was like being bombarded by larger than life forces. Actually, there were times when I felt I was wrestling with the Devil himself.

As this crisis continued unabated, I developed symptoms not unlike physical indigestion, except in this case the root cause was psycho-spiritual. What was I to do? For the sake of inner harmony was I supposed to leave this new teaching and cease my spiritual practices? Was I to go back to sleep and forget what had happened during and following that epiphany experience? Even before I asked, I knew this was not an option. I could no more forget the Love that had embraced me nor the Power that had quickened me than I could turn back history.

This inner upheaval was brought on initially by my encounter with Spirit—followed by the discovery of the Science of Mind teaching. The present crisis seemed the result of old established beliefs in direct opposition to these two new events in my life. *I wondered how I could be so consciously aware and absolutely certain that I was being divinely guided and, at the same time, have these fears, misgivings, and suspicions appear with such force.* Nonetheless, from this inner conflict I learned some interesting things about myself—that even though there were aspects ready, eager, and even ecstatic at the possibility of following the 'Light,' there were other aspects *very much afraid to let go of the old.*

I felt strongly that the ideas I was being introduced to in the Science of Mind augmented basic Scripture and the teachings of Jesus, yet these newer interpretations of truth were too far removed from my former beliefs to be understood and accepted by them. One of those beliefs was an early indoctrination into the 'sin and separation' story. Evidently my new truth—of God, Omnipresent—was not compatible with my old truth. Actually, before being embraced by this Holy Presence I might not have understood these new teachings, but now they were like manna from heaven.

I understood, in the midst of all the churning inside, that there was only one way out of my present dilemma—and that was through it! To assuage my fears and concerns about what was happening, instead of seeing this as a battle between powerful psycho-spiritual forces, which of course it was, I began to view this as reprogramming and updating my old belief system. Not until I finally surrendered to the wisdom of Spirit to sort out this difficulty was I guided to slow the pace and ease the intensity of my prayers and affirmations. Soon thereafter, I began to feel at peace in my soul. Perhaps God was waiting for me to get my ego and my fears out of the 'divine circuits.'

* * *

For generations, my family history has been rooted in Southern Baptist doctrine. I don't recall anyone in my family ever taking issue with the church's interpretation of Scripture; if they did, they kept it to themselves. My early ideas of God were vague and nebulous—of a being not unlike an old man in the sky—remote and far, far away—not of this physical world and completely separated from his creation. This concept of God left me feeling isolated and alone. Unable to discern the deeper spiritual truths in the *Bible*, I soon lost interest in trying.

Recalling my early church experience, I saw how heavily I had been indoctrinated into the second creation story (Genesis: Chapter 3) the story of Eve's disobedience to God, described as the "fall." The message that was reiterated—time and again—was the stigma of "sin" forever cast against all humanity through Eve's disobedience. This story painted a picture in my mind's eye of a judgmental and wrathful male figure. The first creation story told in Genesis: chapters 1 and 2, telling us we are "created in the image and likeness of God....and given dominion…," was so completely upstaged and overshadowed by this second story of creation, that it's message was psychologically lost on me.

Suddenly I saw this second creation story in a glaring, new light. The incredible influence of this narrative—its truth misplaced, misunderstood, and misinterpreted for centuries as a negative worldview of women is beyond measure. No doubt this story has wrecked havoc on the psyches of men and women—keeping both from seeing a greater truth—that as male and female, we are first, last, and always God's beloved creation. I no longer think of God as a male figure, rather a Spirit encompassing all the elements of both natures—male and female.

Both creation stories describe important spiritual truths; however, they have not always been taught in the proper order. If I had first been told that I was a child of God—and then told of my human shortcomings, at least I would have had my identity established. If I had first known I was divinely fashioned and given dominion over my life would I not be better equipped to move beyond my human failings—to love and forgive others and myself, and to live a more Christ-like life? The immense potential of the human spirit nurtured in such an environment staggers the imagination.

* * *

Before the conflict between my old and new beliefs, what knowledge I had of the unconscious was miniscule and pretty much confined to the role of maintaining and sustaining the health and well being of my physical body at cellular/molecular levels. Now I was anxious to learn more about the nature of the unconscious mind. I had heard of Dr. Carl Jung and the research he and his colleagues were doing in this field. From the library I found the book, *A Primer of Jungian Psychology,* by Calvin S. Hall and Vernon J. Nordby. Jung's theory was that the unconscious mind is not only a repository of one's personal thoughts, feelings, perceptions, and experiences from birth to the present moment, but also a vast reservoir of the "collective unconscious" of the human race. Within this "collective unconscious" is contained all the world's knowledge and history as well as all human experiences, including those borne of pain, ignorance, fears, and superstition.

My encounter with Spirit was an event that took place somewhere beyond my conscious mind: therefore my conclusion was that the unconscious must also be the place where we meet God. From Ernest Holmes' teachings I learned the role of the conscious mind was to filter out the extraneous, contradictory material of the unconscious—allowing us to choose one idea or belief at a time from its immense resources. The role of the conscious mind was to take the initiative, choose, and make decisions, while the role of the unconscious mind was to support those initiatives, choices, and decisions. Contemplating the depth, breadth, and power of the unconscious, and the intricate interplay between these two aspects of the human mind, I was awestruck at the handiwork of God. I felt, as did the writer of Psalms 139:14, when he penned these words, "I will praise thee; for I am fearfully and wonderfully made…"

* * *

In my eagerness to see changes in my life I had put myself in an untenable situation. All too quickly I learned why the unconscious mind was designed to remain unconscious; that is, until such time as the conscious mind is adequately equipped to handle the many contradictions found there. Still, this rather traumatic episode proved both a revelation—and a renovation—of my psyche. When the conflict subsided I felt my new-found faith had successfully quelled my remaining doubts and put my suspicions to rest. I had to wonder if this turbulent period was a kind of initiation to determine if I had the faith and courage to stay the course.

Fortified with the growing sense of God as an ever-present Spirit, I began to feel that my newly developing spiritual life was on solid ground, but beyond that, I had no idea what challenges lay ahead. I had yet to learn that my habituated thought patterns and the emotional energies they carried—in spite of my best efforts to abolish the negative ones—would never be entirely eradicated. Ernest Holmes discovered, from his own experience, that they "return with monotonous regularity"—to be dealt with again and again! Why?—because our core beliefs, influenced by society, religion, environment, and ancestral lineage over a lifetime, become fixed patterns. Still, I felt, with continuing prayers and affirmations, those destructive patterns could eventually be healed.

* * *

This desire to have a more intimate relationship with God meant I not only had to forfeit every belief that denied that possibility, I also had to develop the discipline of daily contemplation and prayer. This determination to change my life gave my old beliefs no choice but to protest. A contested battle was inevitable! My, my, my! What an introduction to the territorial nature of some of my core beliefs! This "battle" was a major hurdle and proved essential to my spiritual growth. Yet I doubt I could have survived had I not experienced God as a loving Presence *before this upheaval.* Had I the presence of mind to ask Spirit to steady me in this endeavor I might have escaped the storm of conflicting ideas and beliefs that beset me. On reflection I see this event, not as the forces of good and evil warring within me—but rather a face-to-face confrontation between my earlier, rather limited concepts of truth and my later more-expanded understanding of *those same truths.*

* * *

Continuing my inquiry into the field of the unconscious I found a book called *Games People Play* written by Dr. Eric Berne, M.D. published in 1964. He coined the phrase "transactional analysis" to describe how people interact with each other. A follow-up book, *I'm Okay—You're Okay—A Practical Guide to Transactional Analysis* by Dr. Thomas Harris, M.D. was published in 1967. Both books were on the Best Seller list for months, but back then I was not particularly interested in this subject. However, following the battle of my beliefs, I was now open to further exploration of these ideas. Fortunately for me, I found a condensed version of transactional analysis in a little pamphlet titled *Introduce Yourself to Transactional Analysis, A TA Primer* by Leonard Campos and Paul McCormick.

The pamphlet was written to assist teenagers and adults in their "individual growth and also in the improvement of our social institutions." It outlined in layman's terms a non-technical description of the theory and practice of transactional analysis (TA). Suddenly I had before me a simple and practical way to better understand my psychological makeup. On the pamphlet cover were three circles, one sitting on top of the other. Within the top circle was a large Capital P, in the middle circle a Capital A, and in the bottom circle a Capital C. These circle drawings, referred to as P.A.C., gave the reader "a diagram of a human being." The authors explained that "Everyone has three parts, or persons, within himself: a Parent, an Adult, and a Child. These parts are known technically as ego states" and "these ego states are like voices in you."

"The Parent in you feels and believes in the same ways your mother and father, or whoever raised you, did. Your Adult is the part that uses facts to make decisions, and your Child has the same feelings and ways of behaving you had when you were young." Was this true? I decided to check out this concept by listening for the voices of my inner Parent, my inner Adult, and my inner Child. Defining which voice was speaking was easier than I thought. Without question my "Parent" dominated my thought processes. (The voice of my parent also included the authority figures I esteemed, along with the parental and religious 'should' and 'should not's' I had been taught.) Why had I allowed my inner Parent to dominate so much of my thinking? No doubt to win parental approval.

The authors indicated that if one aspect dominated the other two, this would indicate an imbalance in one's psychological development. According to my findings, I was definitely out of balance. Amazed at how this simple formula defined some of the complexities of my inner world, I was now able to see where, in what, and in whom I had placed my faith and belief. Actually, this material felt so pertinent I quietly began the work of reconnecting, a little each day, with my inner Adult—giving her room to breathe and grow and stretch her wings. As a result, by making conscious choices and carefully weighing my decisions, my inner Adult gradually took back control over my mind. Listening also to my inner Child, I began to appreciate her and what must have confused her as a little girl. As for my inner Parent, I think she was ready for a rest.

This concept of "Inner Parent, Adult, and Child," gave me a new and different framework for relating to my human personality. I appreciated knowing that those tapes sometimes playing inside my head were made very early in my life and *were not the actual details of events that happened in the past but rather my feelings and interpretations of those events.* In retrospect, I saw that both my inner Parent and my inner Child had often blocked the authority and expression of my inner Adult. Not only had I ceded my "adult" power to my "inner parent" and certain authority figures, but also to fears and demands of my "inner child." I now understood that, as an adult, I was to reason out the truth in my own mind and heart—and to silence those inner and outer voices that tried to tell me otherwise.

* * *

In my upbringing my father had played a passive role, my mother the dominant role. She was a no-nonsense lady, determined to see that her girls "turned out right" (whatever that meant in her mind). I believe she really did know what was best for my two younger sisters and me. Unfortunately, her style was to lecture. She didn't believe in dialogue or lengthy discussions on any subject that affected me. Too often her monologues sounded like sermons and, as a result, I learned to tune them out. Because of our age differences I cannot speak for her parenting of my two younger sisters, but from my own experience I was not allowed to express a different opinion. I was to listen politely—and of course obey.

Although there was little real dialogue between us before I married, the day I married our relationship changed. Instantly I became an adult in her eyes. She was a good mother and mother-in-law, never offering advice unless asked. I'll always be grateful to both parents for their dedication to truth as they understood it—and for rearing me the best they knew how. They were firm in their parental role, but also fair and just. Above all, I knew they loved me. To blame them, my religion, society, or anyone else for my early confusion over spiritual matters would not only be unfair but would mask the issue at hand—that of taking full responsibility for my life as it was then, and as it is now. From a new understanding of these inner "ego states," my adult could finally take control of my psyche.

Chapter 6

"…. as thou hast believed, so be it done unto thee."
Matt. 8:13

Jesus is said to have made the above statement to a Roman centurion who had asked him to heal his ailing servant. In their brief conversation, Jesus marveled at the depth of this man's faith and belief, saying, "…I have not found so great faith, no, not in Israel." Then he said to the centurion, "…Go thy way; and as thou hast believed, so be it done unto thee. And his servant was healed in the selfsame hour." (Matt. 8:10-13) Until now I had not considered this story anything other than an amazing account of Jesus' ability to heal. While I had seen the importance of the centurion's faith and belief in Jesus, I had failed to grasp, in this simple phrase, the far-reaching implications of a more subtle truth.

The law of "as thou hast believed, so be it done unto thee" was in place for both the centurion and for Jesus: For the centurion, because he believed in Jesus' power to heal—and for Jesus, because he knew himself to be imbued with the Holy Spirit. I was familiar with the teachings of Jesus—but had been blind to the underlying spiritual principles embedded in them. Ernest Holmes, in his search for the spiritual principles in Jesus' teachings, recognized in this particular statement a law that automatically responds to our beliefs *to the degree of our faith in those beliefs*. He saw this as a mental/spiritual law, *that was not only universal and timeless—but also neutral—and as applicable to us today as it was to the centurion two thousand years ago.*

Dr. Holmes also understood that this law wasn't limited to our belief and faith in God, but applied to *everything* we deeply believed to be true. This revelation enabled him to see just how subtly this law operates in our lives. For instance, if our faith and beliefs are, for the most part, optimistic in nature, this law will naturally reflect that optimism in our circumstances and affairs. Likewise, if our faith and beliefs lean more to a pessimistic view of life, this same law will respond like Murphy's Law, reflecting that pessimism in our experiences.

* * *

My only knowledge of spiritual laws as they concerned human behavior had been limited to the Ten Commandments in the *Old Testament* and the Two Commandments in the *New Testament*. The Ten Commandments appeared to be an edict handed down to Moses from some great God for the people of Israel—of *what one <u>is not to do</u> as children of God*—while the Two Commandments given by Jesus spelled out *what one <u>is to do</u> to live in harmony with God, our neighbor, and ourselves.* Although I wasn't sure in my teen years what I believed God to be, I did feel there was some infinite source of wisdom in charge of the universe. Within that context, I had a vague sense of divine cosmic law and order. Still I couldn't connect the judgmental God of the *Old Testament* with the loving Spirit of God exemplified by the life of Jesus in the *New Testament*. The Holy Ghost was a total enigma!

Many of my beliefs had been molded 'piecemeal,' perhaps even happenstance, from early parental, societal, and religious conditioning, as well as from childhood fears and misperceptions. According to Dr. Jung's research, these impressions, ideas, thoughts, feelings, and attitudes—*true and false*—had been meticulously stored in my unconscious mind—forming the basis of my beliefs. Having experienced God as a loving spiritual Presence, I was still basing my judgments on what I could sense with my outer faculties—what I could touch, taste, and smell and what I could see, hear, and understand. It was much easier to trust the evidence of my outer senses than to try and comprehend the more subtle realms of being. There was, after all, a practicality in rational thinking that was believable. Gradually though, I began to feel more deeply the truth of Spirit as the underlying life of my life—of all life; and that in God, we actually do live and move and have our being.

* * *

Having relied on my outer senses, I wondered how this law of "as thou hast believed..." had actually played out in my early church experience. As a teen, I felt the focus of my Southern Baptist church was more a judgment of my 'sins' (translated—'ignorance') than on God's love and forgiveness. It seemed to me the church had a philosophic bent for over-emphasizing the sin/sinner story. Told every Sunday that I was a lowly sinner but that Jesus loved me anyway, I was not told the glorious truth that I was, first and foremost, a beloved child of a loving Father-Mother God.

As a young adult I put the issue of God and truth in the category of "unknowable mysteries"—which of course it was—to perhaps ponder at some later date. In the meantime I lived more or less on the surface of my life, engrossed in the physical and material world, in my personal and immediate needs, and later in the needs of my family. And life was good. Not until mid-life, when faced with some of life's more difficult questions around aging, disease, and death, did I need answers that couldn't be found in my physical world. As those deeper issues arose I met again my earlier nemesis—my many unanswered questions about life and God.

This must have been my unconscious prayer, for soon thereafter, I was spiritually awakened, and transformed in the process. Once I had this glorious vision of God as a holy Presence, I knew I was 'the beloved'—as we all are. Still, I wanted to know more of the nature of God. Led to the Science of Mind teachings, I discovered God to be both "Love" and "Law." I also discovered the spiritual principles of Love and Law embedded in the teachings and healing ministry of Jesus.

* * *

How had this law of "it is done unto us as we believe..." affected other areas of my life, I wondered? My thoughts turned to the crisis at hand and what beliefs I may have entertained around a belief in disease and my susceptibility to this particular one. Had I consciously believed I would someday contract rheumatoid arthritis? Of course not! In fact, when I came upon this law of "as thou hast believed, so be it done unto thee" in relation to this disease I was angry and defensive. Feeling in some way responsible for creating this disease in my body, I immediately began searching for ways to exonerate my involvement. As I began to work through my feelings, the idea of guilt, blame, or even responsibility became irrelevant since, at the time, I had not been conscious of my part.

Of course, there were many complex factors contributing to the development of this disease, *not the least of which was my faith and belief in disease itself.* How far back in my family ancestry, and in the collective consciousness of human history, had this particular pattern of disease established itself in our DNA? I didn't know, but I did know that since time began humans have believed in the reality of disease and suffering as an inevitable part of the human experience. Had we faith and belief in God as an overriding healing power and presence in the world might we enjoy good health and avoid disease altogether? This higher truth of God, All-powerful, All-knowing, and Everywhere present has never been part of our belief system. While we pray to God to ease our suffering, disease remains a reality in the collective unconscious of the entire human race. And so "it is done unto us as we believe."

Now, as my belief in God as a healing Presence was beginning to take hold, was it possible to overcome my underlying belief in disease and eventually experience a full physical healing? Although that profound encounter in 1972 had healed me in so many ways, it had not healed me in all ways. I was healed in my mind and spirit to the truth of God as an everywhere present Reality, and healed in my body of the excruciating pain I had experienced at the onset of this disease. That much healing seemed more than I could have hoped for.

I accepted the verdict that rheumatoid arthritis was incurable and sought medication to keep my joints mobile and pretty much pain-free. Rather than focusing on a physical healing, I spent all of my time and energy seeking after spiritual understanding. Deeply engrossed in my spiritual studies I never thought to ask Spirit for a complete physical healing. Perhaps I thought that once I reached a certain level of spiritual development I would naturally experience a physical healing. All the while, at unconscious levels, I was deeply immersed in this collective belief in disease—with all its ramifications. As a result arthritis has remained present in my body, but so far without severe crippling.

This idea of innate good health as a divine gift had a ring of truth to it; however, the disease evident in my sister and in me looked and felt far more real than any belief I could envision of our perfect health. While I wanted to be free in my own mind from the effects of this world belief in disease and be healed of it, I knew it would take more faith and belief in God as my perfect health than I had accumulated thus far. Nonetheless, I felt that if our world belief in disease could ever be countered by a greater realization of God as our Source and Substance, the power of disease would gradually weaken its hold over humanity.

Ernest Holmes believed in the power of prayer to heal. In a booklet titled *Path of Discovery – The Story of Ernest Holmes*, (prepared in 1987 by Scott Awbrey, of the United Church of Religious Science) I learned more about Holmes' passion for God and his lifelong search for truth. Ernest had studied *The Holy Bible* and other spiritual literature, as well as *Emerson's Essays*, and the lectures of Judge Thomas Troward, a Scotsman and eighteenth-century judge in India. From these and other sources he concluded that there was a universal law that could be called upon for healing—one that anyone could use, independent of any particular religious faith. This booklet quotes Ernest as saying, "I intuitively felt that the affirmation of God's goodness would heal the sick. I began with the belief that God is all and I never departed from it. If we do not like our outer circumstances, conditions, or our personality, the place to begin to change is right within our own mind."

This became the premise of his philosophy, as outlined in his book, *The Science of Mind.* Dr. Holmes felt sure that, through the practice of prayers and affirmations, we could build enough faith and belief in God as the Giver of Life—and in ourselves as the recipients of that Life—to bring about a state of health in our minds and in our bodies, even in the midst of serious health problems. He demonstrated this ability to heal human conditions through prayer, and taught others to do the same. Had I not been exposed to the truth of God as an Ever-present Reality, I might never have found this healing philosophy.

We don't need to validate our belief in disease as a reality of human life; there is enough pain and suffering in the world to prove that point. Besides, there had been little, if any, verifiable data or scientific evidence to support any anecdotal claim of healing through spiritual means. My question was: "If good health is our innate nature, why are we not experiencing it?" The answer seemed to lie in this phrase "as thou hast believed, so be it done unto thee." As human beings, feeling separated from our Spiritual Source—from the Intelligence and Wisdom that meant us to have health and have it abundantly—we have made ourselves vulnerable to a belief in its opposite—disease.

At this point, I was sure of two things: that Spirit, as a holy Presence, could heal any disease, even one pronounced incurable—and that I was currently unable to rise above a world belief in disease to experience my own healing. I had met a most perplexing paradox, an apparent contradiction in terms—a belief, on one level, that disease is real and, on another level, that health is real. I'm finally satisfied that both are real, the distinction being that disease is a relative truth—*and therefore subject to change*—while God as our life and our health is the ultimate, absolute, and changeless truth—if we can only believe!

* * *

In my studies I was learning more about how this subtle law of "it is done unto us as we believe" worked in actual practice. For example, if we believe in the power and presence of God to heal us, the law will work according to that belief—by working to heal us. On the other hand, if we do not believe in the healing power of prayer, in the love of God, or in our own worthiness, this law will work, *again according to our belief,* by appearing *not to work.* This law of "it is done unto me as I believe..." is always working for me or against me by the thoughts I entertain, by the words I speak, and by my underlying faith and belief—either in God as the ground of my being, or in a human condition called disease.

Some time after I began an inquiry into this law, a wonderful insight came forward—that what I had earlier believed I could have, what I believed I could do, and what I believed I could be had all come to pass! Likewise, what I had not believed I could have, could do, or could be had not come to pass. Thus, I only had to look at my life's experiences to see what my beliefs were. God has given us dominion over our lives so that we are free to choose which beliefs to cultivate and which ones to discard.

* * *

This law of "it is done unto us as we believe" manifested in other areas of my life as well. Thinking of how, as a child, I attributed a superior intelligence to all authority figures, I realized as an adult that I still held some of those same beliefs. Not only that—but somewhere along the way, my glorification of the "human intellect" had translated into an unconscious belief in the superiority of the "male intellect." (Although not all authority figures were male in that era, most were.)

Also, in my early studies of American and European history I became intrigued and greatly impressed by the accomplishments of those who had given the world such a rich history. I admired the accomplishments of gifted people and their tremendous contributions to society, in the vision of our nation's forefathers, as well as the advancement in science and technology, and in the arts. Indeed, I became so enamored with the great statesmen, scientists, as well as the literary and artistic geniuses of the Western world, I came to believe that human intelligence alone had advanced our civilization. I gave God none of the credit.

Now I wondered why I had taken such pride in the human intellect and had given so little credit to God—or, for that matter, to my own intelligence. Why had I been so proud to be part of a culture that was spectacularly successful in its intellectual endeavors when I had not even been a contributor? I had not only failed to appreciate and honor my own intelligence, I had failed to acknowledge God as the One Intelligence behind all human intelligence. Finally, I understood that the human intellect was not meant to overshadow the development of our psychological and spiritual nature—nor was it intended to usurp the role of God in our lives.

After reading Betty Freidan's book, *The Feminine Mystique,* I was suddenly aware of an awful truth—that after all these years, I was still psychologically under the influence of male authority figures. Awakening to a truth I already knew but had ignored—that for over two thousand years society and religion have operated under a patriarchal system of male domination—emotions of rage suddenly broke through my passive exterior. The origin of this rage was the stark realization that this collective mind-set had caused me as a young woman to *feel less than*—in the eyes of God and the world.

The "feminine mystique" Friedan was referring to in her book was this patriarchal lack of understanding of the basic needs of women. She writes, "It is my thesis that the core of the problem for women today is not sexual but a problem of identity—a stunting or evasion of growth that is perpetuated by the feminine mystique." She goes on to say,

> "…as the Victorian culture did not permit women to accept or gratify their basic sexual needs, our culture does not permit women to accept or gratify their basic need to grow and fulfill their potentialities as human beings, a need which is not solely defined by their sexual role." (*The Feminine Mystique*, p. 77)

My anger was directed at this patriarchal belief system for perpetuating this not-so-subtle myth of male dominion in today's world. Society and religion have always assumed *that women would be completely and totally fulfilled* in the roles assigned to them as homemakers, wives, and mothers. This was perhaps true in our beginning history, when men needed to be strong hunters and guardians of their clan, and women took care of the basic needs of their families. Our problems are no longer tribal, but global. The talents and skills of both men and women, working side by side in every field of endeavor, are needed to find workable solutions, not only in our local communities, but also on those larger issues affecting our state and nation, our neighbors abroad, and around the globe.

How had this myth of male domination developed in the first place—and in the second place, why had women blindly accepted it? I believe the idea of male dominion has its roots in the "Garden of Eden" story, with the image of God as a male God, and Eve, disobedient and sinful, leading Adam down the primrose path. Over the millennia both men and women have accepted this patriarchal view as 'the Gospel truth'—thinking of it as the divine right of men to have dominion over women. Another societal decision, still largely uncontested, is that married and single women who work outside the home automatically receive less pay than their male counterparts.

Whereas, I had previously paid little attention, now I gave a lot of thought to these facts and my feelings about them. In a world where more women have to work outside the home to feed their family, this state of affairs is no longer acceptable. Even today, as women seek equal status with men in the world of human affairs—in the business world, in the voting booth, or in the religious life of the church—they are often met with strong opposition, based on Biblical beliefs and established prejudices. Though women have made great strides toward obtaining equal rights, *they still do not have all of their rights!* Women who fought for and attained their rights have endured harassment and discrimination by their male peers. Yet, despite efforts to impose artificial ceilings for women, many have made their mark.

Young women today, whose dreams have been nurtured and supported by those who believed in their greater potential, are moving past old barriers and succeeding in ways unimagined a generation ago. For the majority of women of my generation our patriarchal society and religion has effectively kept us "in our place." This includes the right of women to make personal decisions (as men do for themselves) that affect their life and the life of their families. In this day and age I cannot accept the claim that men have been given dominion by God over the rights and freedom of women.

I seriously question a religion that ordains man as the sole authority in the family when domestic violence, incest, and sexual assault continue today as serious crimes against wives and daughters. Why do women continue to take abuse from fathers, husbands, and/or bosses? Why do women not stand up to such abuse? No doubt they feel trapped, powerless, and vulnerable to further mistreatment—and even made to feel guilty for their mistreatment. Why, I wondered, have we given away our natural birthright and our inherent power to men? Have we forgotten that we, too, are creations of a loving God, given the same inalienable rights as men to live our lives fully and freely?

Indeed, why are we still deferring to men and allowing them to control our personal and communal health and welfare? Our world has suffered enough from the cumulative effects of male domination. This male mind-set continues to downplay a woman's right to be all that she can be. So ingrained over the centuries is this manifesto that few think to question the incongruity of it. I believe God meant men and women to value and respect each other's gifts in all human relationships—mutually supportive in the family and equally compensated in the work place. Perhaps an equal partnership is the next step in our development towards becoming more fully human.

Chapter 7

"As a man thinketh in his heart, so is he."
Proverbs 23:7

Here was another important truth similar to, yet quite different from, Jesus's statement, "As thou hast believed, so be it done unto you." "As thou hast believed…" seemed more a mental and conscious activity while "as a man thinketh in his heart..." appeared to be more an emotional, unconscious reaction. Although I was familiar with both Bible verses, I had failed to grasp the deeper, personal implications in them. I now found this idea extremely provocative and more than a little disturbing—'that what I am thinking in my heart is who I really am.' Could I actually discover who I am by simply looking at my thoughts and feelings?

Prior to 1972 and my awakening experience, I had hardly known my own inner thought processes. I paid little heed to the running dialogue going on in my head and heart. Preoccupied with daily tasks, I had often given free rein to what seemed like the idle ramblings of fragmented, innocuous thoughts and feelings. When I discovered that my thoughts and feelings were not without substance and power, I was shocked. I soon learned they were a major force to be reckoned with.

On the cover of every issue of the *Science of Mind* magazine is this phrase "Change your thinking; change your life"—a bold statement that declares the healing power of the mind through right thinking, right speaking, and right believing. The premise is that we can create healthier, more harmonious lives by *consciously* choosing to think more positively. The Science of Mind teachings became the door, not only to my deeper understanding of God and the principles Jesus taught, but also of how to apply these principles for healing. Considering the negative aspects of my past thinking, there was no denying I had carried around some unhealthy ideas about life in general—and about myself in particular.

I was my own example of how one's thoughts and feelings work "for" or "against" oneself. I began to see a definite mind/body connection—and how my thoughts and emotions, as energy vibrations, continually play, dance, and weave their way among the cells and many systems of my body. Once I thought it through, it didn't seem too far-fetched to believe that negative mental and emotional energies could, over time, accumulate to eventually disrupt the immune system—setting the stage for disease.

Another Bible verse addressed the power of negative emotions to affect our lives. From Ephesians 4:26 we are told—"....let not the sun go down upon your wrath." Again, like so many other truths, this one had escaped me. I neither understood the gravity of holding onto negative energy—nor what these destructive patterns can do to body and soul. This verse was speaking an important truth—that unless we release our mental and emotional baggage each day, through prayer and forgiveness for ourselves and others, these negative energies will remain with us.

Could the negative emotions I had held onto for so long be a possible cause for the disease of rheumatoid arthritis in my body? No doubt there were other contributing factors beyond my knowledge and understanding, but not finding healthy ways to release negative thoughts and feelings was certainly a major one. Perhaps I could have bypassed much pain and suffering if I had understood and complied with the underlying truth given in this Bible verse.

I already knew my propensity to nurse hurts and grievances longer than I should. Like a vice, my mind could lock on to any issue I felt strongly about, sometimes building enormous amounts of energy as I silently argued my case—not knowing that, if not released appropriately and in a timely manner, these energies could become lethal. Was my dislike for confrontation a factor here? Life, after all, is meant to be expressed. Yet, I almost always avoided expressing my point of view when it differed from the majority. Keeping my thoughts and feelings inside was an attempt to preserve the peace around me—yet there was anything but peace within me.

God has given each of us the power to consciously choose the direction of our life, at least to some degree. In assessing my conscious choices, I had done okay! However, my ignorance of this underlying law of my life—that at unconscious levels of thought and feeling I had habitually sat in critical judgment of others and myself, was a revelation. Had I been awake to the truth that "as I think in my heart, so am I," I would have searched out ways to be more kind and loving. Fortunately, it is never too late to learn to apply those universal laws and principles that govern life at unconscious levels—to which we are all subject, whether we believe or not.

* * *

I had two revelatory dreams during this chaotic period. Without their timely appearance, I might have ceded the psychological battle taking place in the deeper recesses of my mind and been tempted to put aside my search for greater understanding. Yet both dreams became signposts on my path—a path that now seemed full of potholes. One of those dreams recurred throughout childhood and once as an adult.

> **The dream:** I was walking down a street when I became aware of a dark figure following me. This figure was wearing a long, black cloak and a large black hat pulled down over its face. When I walked, "it" walked; when I ran, "it" ran; when I stopped, "it" stopped. The dream always ended when I tried to scream but couldn't. This attempt to scream always awakened me.

The last time I had this dream the scene shifted, and for the first time I decided to turn and face the figure, to see just who was chasing me. When I turned, "it" raised its head and I looked into a face so indistinct that it could hardly be called a face. Yet I saw a definite smile—and in that instant the face and figure vanished before my eyes. I deduced that it was nothing more than a fear-figment of my imagination, without any substance in and of itself. Suddenly I understood the truth in Franklin Roosevelt's statement, "the only thing we have to fear is fear itself." Evidently that was the message of this dream! After all, the dream had repeated itself over the years until I finally took some initiative to turn and face my adversary. This dream has never returned.

The second dream took place during a quiet time of meditation, not while sleeping. It felt more like a vision than a dream. As I understand dreams, they're usually a sequence of events. This one revealed two vivid pictures. These images are as clear today in my mind's eye as they were when presented to me in the mid-70's.

> **The Vision:** From a dream state, I was standing in a large pine-paneled living room in a cabin in the woods. Looking northward out a large picture window, I saw a small figure standing in a low-lying area some fifty yards away, almost hidden in the shadow of tall evergreen trees. Although I was unable to identify this figure from such a distance, I understood it represented me. Beyond this figure I saw a dark, narrow, winding river flowing east to west diagonally across the landscape.

Suddenly the scene changed and I was no longer an observer looking out a picture window. I was now this figure I'd seen standing in the shadows—with the flowing river directly in front of me. Looking across the river, I saw a robed figure with outstretched arms, bathed in light, standing on a small knoll facing me. My first guess was that this was Jesus. A short distance behind him loomed a great mountain that dominated the background landscape. Instead of having the customary aspects of a mountain (trees, ridges, canyons, and perhaps a cap of snow), the rather stark terrain was in earth tones of tans and browns with large and small boulders scattered about. Behind its peak, completing the picture, was a radiant, golden light.

This river effectively blocked my passage to the opposite shore. From where I stood, I couldn't see a bridge over the river, a route around it, or anything like a boat to ferry me across. That meant I could either enter the river and swim across or remain where I was. Although I feared entering what I perceived to be dangerous waters, nevertheless, I knew I must get to the other side. While this vision looked like a major physical challenge—crossing a dangerous river and then climbing a formidable mountain—I knew it was not a physical journey.

These images were about meeting the Master Jesus on my journey to God. Undoubtedly, this journey would challenge my deepest fears, yet to undertake it would be immensely rewarding. Plainly, this sojourn would be nothing less than a mental, emotional, and spiritual odyssey through uncharted waters and across unmapped landscapes.

Metaphorically I was looking at my life—at my present status and my possible future. The message could not have been clearer—there was a mountain to climb—but first, a dark and foreboding river to cross! Fortunately, standing on that knoll across the way was "Someone," far greater than my little human sense of self, offering strength and encouragement. Although I believed the obstacles before me, symbolized by the river and the mountain, would not be impossible to overcome, I knew they would test my mettle in every possible way. To begin with, just in the figurative swim across that river, I would have to face up to, and then face down, a multitude of unnamed fears, requiring greater resources than I possessed at that moment.

In those early years of learning how to follow the "Light of Spirit," I felt caught in the currents and eddies of my old belief system more than a few times. It felt like old bottles breaking apart and new bottles being molded to fit my expanded ideas of God. Throughout this process, I held fast to my new sense of God as an indwelling Spirit. I affirmed that truth in my prayers as though it was my life preserver (which indeed it was). Daily, I sought to cleanse my mind and heart of unworthy thoughts and feelings, replacing them with the truest, most positive thoughts I could muster—all the while, asking Spirit for guidance and direction.

The message in both dreams was two-fold: I realized, to grow spiritually, I must overcome the irrational, illogical fears that stood on my path. At the same time, both dreams implied a potential inner reserve, a hidden strength, capable of conquering and dispelling those fears. My role was to find ways to access those potential reserves and tap into my inner strengths to dissolve the power of those fears. My course of action was continued prayers and truth affirmations. These activities had already become part of my daily work—not only to find inspiration and healing for my mind, and loving, healing thoughts for my heart—but now also to build an inner reserve of strength and courage. Almost imperceptibly, an inner strength gradually began to show forth—a strength I had not known I possessed.

I wondered why my mind was drawn to focus, not on the positive good around me, but on critical judgments of what was happening around me. In a wonderful analogy in the Bible, Jesus uses the "Parable of the "Sower" to liken the word of truth to that of a seed. In this parable we are told that seeds of truth are sometimes sown on ground that is neither prepared nor tended and, therefore, they can never reach maturity, but seeds of truth sown in good ground will bring forth a rich harvest. (Mark: 4:14-20)

The parables of Jesus suddenly took on new meaning when I came across a little book, *Learn to Live, The Meaning of the Parables,* by Dr. Ervin Seale. In his preface, he says, "The Parables, significantly, not only illustrate what human conduct should be; they reveal, in their subtle way, how to do the thing that we see should be done.

> He writes, The parable (of the sower) stresses the truth that the seed falls indiscriminately from the hand of the sower upon all types of soil. The seed is reality; but reality is always qualified and conditioned by the mind that regards it. As the rain falls upon the just and the unjust, and the sun shines upon the good and the evil with equal generosity, so the seeds of truth fall upon the variable minds of men (and women). The different kinds of mind among men (and women) are like the different kinds of soil in the parable.

Picturing my mind as a garden helped me understand that whatever seeds I planted and carefully cultivated would grow and bring forth fruit according to their kind. If I plant seeds of love and truth and nurture their growth, I will harvest abundant good. Likewise, if I plant and nurture seeds of anger, fear, envy, resentment, or jealousy, my harvest will return to me those same seeds fully-grown. Even if I plant good seeds, but allow weeds of doubt and fear to grow among them, I will reap a poor harvest. I had heard this particular parable often in my youth but had never understood the depth of meaning as it pertained to me—and what kinds of seeds I was planting in my mind.

As I carefully considered this concept, I noticed that I must have planted—deliberately and consciously—some good seeds as well as some bad seeds, but there were other types for which I couldn't account. Had some seeds entered unannounced and unbidden, without my conscious choosing, on the winds of public opinion? Even so, wasn't it my responsibility to stand guard at the entrance to my mind, to prevent unwanted seeds from entering and taking root?

* * *

Another beautiful metaphor of the inner workings of mind and heart was the image of a loom, which I found in my readings. I loved this symbol because it so graphically explained what seemed inexplicable. Our subconscious mind can be likened to a "loom" that takes the threads of our thoughts and the colors of our feelings and, from them, weaves the patterns of our experiences. This loom works ceaselessly, taking every thought and every feeling, never questioning our choice of color or design.

Both metaphors—the garden and the loom—vividly illustrate how our subconscious mind operates as a creative force. Indeed, as the master gardener and the weaver of my life I must choose with care and discrimination. Armed now with this knowledge, I realized that the thoughts, feelings, and experiences I had created out of ignorance could actually be uncreated and recreated according to a more perfect truth. Indeed, how I had chosen to respond to life's vicissitudes had had a limiting effect on my mind and heart and, I believe, on my physical health as well. How exhilarating to realize I could plant new seeds in my mind-garden closer to the truth. I could also select threads of rich, vibrant color and texture to weave a more beautiful design for my life—even at this late stage.

Actually, with deep gratitude I began to appreciate that I had actually planted many good seeds and woven some beautiful tapestries in my lifetime. My marriage, my family, my friends, my home, and my environment were great blessings. Again, what I thought I could be, what I thought I could do, and what I thought I could have had manifested in my life. Yet I had to wonder—if my conscious and subconscious mind had been relatively free of negativity—if my eyes could have seen and my ears heard earlier—if my heart had been opened sooner to the unconditional love and presence of Spirit—what greater good might have been accomplished?

As I understood the creative power of my subconscious mind to work for or against my desires, hopes, and dreams, I diligently replanted my mind-garden with positive, loving, healthy seed-thoughts. For my loom, I carefully chose new threads of truth in luscious colors of radiant love, light, and beauty. Finally comprehending a higher truth—that God had given me sovereignty over my own soul, with the freedom to say "yes" or "no" to life, I saw with greater clarity the phenomenal power of my thoughts and feelings to create both good and ill in the world.

Slowly I began to extricate myself from many of the issues that had caused so much anxiety. My greatest worries had been my young sister's illness and my concern for the physical and emotional welfare of my parents. Working with prayer, I was finally able to release my fears for Judy, as well as for my parents, placing them in God's hands. Prayer was equally effective in releasing each of our children—newly married or away at college by then—to become mature adults. After all, they had grown beyond the scope of my direct influence. I had no alternative, really, but to let them go and trust in divine guidance.

It was necessary in those early years to let go many of my past beliefs. At times I felt like a trapeze artist in mid-air—letting go of one swing and reaching out for the other. Afraid to let go, afraid not to let go! Actually, I felt as though I was losing my life and, in a sense I was—releasing old, familiar patterns while creating new truths to live by. I found renewed resolve in this statement by Jesus: "For whosoever will save his life shall lose it: and whosoever shall lose his life for my sake shall find it." (Matt. 16:25)

As a Science of Mind student my mantra became "Let go and let God." Not only did I have to let go my old, limited ideas and beliefs about God, but also my limited ideas and beliefs about *everything*. What a pleasant surprise to find that what I had to give up were things I no longer needed or wanted in my life. Two Bible references, especially comforting, were the Twenty-third and Ninety-first Psalms." The following Bible verses also helped me to trust and let go: "With God all things are possible"; "Be still and know that I am God"; and "It is not I, but the Father within, who doeth the work."

The statement, "As a man thinketh in his heart, so is he," was very revealing in the context of how open and closed my own heart was to giving and receiving unconditional love and forgiveness. If I could love God, my neighbor, and myself as God loves me blessings would undoubtedly flow in abundance. However, from an ego state, it is impossible to comprehend what unconditional love is and how to use it indiscriminately. Could this explain why humans suffer heavy, broken, lonely, grieving hearts?

I remember seeing an ancient Egyptian hieroglyph in a museum once in which a human heart was placed opposite a feather on the Scales of Justice. The indication was that to cross over into the after-life one's heart must be as light as a feather. This symbol is a good reminder to hold our burdens lightly, or to let them go entirely. Evidently, a light heart is required of us, not only for entry into the after-life, but for our health and well being in this life as well. Again Jesus said, "Come unto me, all ye that labour and are heavy laden, and I will give you rest. Take my yoke upon you and learn of me; for I am meek and lowly in heart: and ye shall find rest unto your souls. For my yoke is easy, and my burden is light." (Matt. 11:28,29,30)

Since I began my spiritual journey in 1972, I don't know how many times I've asked God to forgive my skewed thinking, my ignorance, my unkind judgments, and all of my other real and imagined lapses. Since I didn't feel unburdened I wasn't quite sure God had heard me or forgiven me. The insight came one day that God forgave me the first time I asked. It was I who had not yet forgiven myself. What a revelation! Why had I been unable to forgive myself? With that question came an immediate answer. I had been unable to love and accept myself in the same way God loves and accepts me—totally and unconditionally—just as I am. I had placed too many prerequisites in the way. The words to an old hymn we used to sing called, "Just as I am," came to mind. Although I was touched by the message in that hymn, I still couldn't comprehend such total acceptance on the part of God for us imperfect souls.

Once I found a place of self-acceptance and self-love in my heart, I began to appreciate that I had done the best I could have in every circumstance, given my level of growth and understanding. As I forgave myself for whatever was troubling my heart, I began to feel healed and at peace. When I looked back, a most amazing thing happened. I couldn't even remember what I had asked forgiveness for! The memory of what that was all about had been miraculously erased, completed, finished. I could only marvel. Today, as I continue my efforts to love and accept myself in the simplest of terms, forgiveness seems easier.

Coming to love and forgive myself has been a long and arduous task and I am hard-pressed to know exactly why this has been so difficult. In my youth, most mornings I awakened in a "sort of gray funk." I assumed this was a normal state of mind. This feeling was hard to dispel, often hanging around well into the day. Once married, that "funky feeling" seemed to dissipate as I became engrossed in my new life as wife and mother.

Now I see more clearly the truth that we are today what we were thinking in our heart yesterday. And tomorrow we will be what we are thinking today. What I was in my heart thirty years ago is not what I have become in my heart today—not perfect but healed in many ways, a happier, more optimistic person and a more loving, caring human being. The key is holding steadfast to the truth of who I am, and who we all are, as beloved by our Creator.

Chapter 8

"And all things, whatsoever ye shall ask
in prayer, believing, ye shall receive.
Matt. 21:22

If the above statement was true I wondered why people didn't always get positive results from their prayers. Indeed, why were prayers sometimes answered and sometimes not? There must be a reason and I was beginning to see it might have more to do with us than with God. In his book, *Healing Words*, Larry Dossey, M.D., indicated this might be the case when he wrote, "Prayer involves more than the power of The Almighty; it is set in motion by human beings, who may be the weak link in an otherwise immensely strong chain. The fact that prayer doesn't work as powerfully and predictably as it might, therefore, may reflect deficiencies not of prayer, but of the pray-er." So, what were those deficiencies and how could one learn to pray correctly?

Stella Terrill Mann, in "*Change Your Life Through Prayer,*" said, "We do not get what we pray for, but what we believe we shall receive." She says that "first we listen to old race fears instead of listening to our own still small voice of faith and common sense. Secondly, we listen to the current race fears around us, and a third way in which we cut off our faith ...is by looking at appearances and judging from them." She goes on to say that we make the mistake of accepting appearances as real and final. I knew this description fitted me; I had had great difficulty getting past my belief in the reality of appearances.

Although I'd heard many prayers in my lifetime, prayer as a personal discipline was strangely unfamiliar. Hearing people pray in church and at weekly prayer meetings didn't make much of an impact on me growing up. Was this because I'd never seen evidence of answered prayer or because I'd never bothered to pray in the first place? I had to say "yes" to both questions. Quite simply, I had trouble believing we could pray and receive what we asked for. Prayer meant communing with God—and to my mind, God was light-years away. Perhaps I didn't believe in prayer because I didn't believe God was a Presence near enough to hear and respond.

When I first discovered the truth that my mind was, in some mysterious way, linked to the mind of God, I immediately saw that prayer was my connection to Spirit. However, following that peak experience, my attempts to establish a reconnection with God through prayer were less than satisfactory. I needed some basic approach to the holy Presence, plus instruction on how to proceed from there. The Science of Mind philosophy provided an outline to follow in asking for God's blessings.

What exactly was the protocol to follow in one's approach to prayer? Were there prayer rules for communicating with Spirit? Contemplating Spirit was a good thing, but was it prayer? First of all, I didn't yet 'get it' that the Law waits for me to ask. This "asking" principle seemed based on the nature of God who has given us freedom of choice—to believe or not believe—to ask or not to ask. When faced with a difficult challenge our options are to go forward on our own merits or ask for what we need and desire, in faith, believing. The question for me was—when was it appropriate to ask for help and when was it better to stand on my own two feet? I decided that prayer was called for whenever I desired something so big I couldn't make it happen on my own merits. Examples—healing my doubting mind, my fearful emotions, or the disease of rheumatoid arthritis in my body.

"Asking" demanded sorting out my thoughts and feelings as to what I actually needed and wanted, then finding a quiet time and place to make those needs and desires known to Spirit. The formula seemed to be to ask, in faith, believing—followed by giving thanks, listening for guidance, and taking action if necessary. Learning to ask came easily enough, but attuning my inner ear to that "still, small voice" has taken a long time to develop.

Having had such an incredible response to prayer in 1972, I knew "something" wondrous happens when, in extreme circumstances, we find ourselves on our knees asking God for help. This profound experience convinced me that when we turn to God, God turns to us. Not since that initial experience have I had that degree of pain—nor that degree of ecstasy in response to simple prayer. Noting the response to one's prayer is in direct proportion to the depth of one's angst, I wondered what to expect from my ordinary everyday prayers.

Looking back on my prayer life, I saw that when I was not in dire emotional or physical pain, responses to my prayers were less dramatic and not always definitive. So subtle and illusive were some responses they often came unnoticed. Once I learned to read the signs, I discovered answers appearing, not only in a variety of ways, but sometimes from the most unlikely people and places. Often I wouldn't recognize the information as being God-directed through the disguises—until I looked back later. When these same ideas kept reappearing over a two or three-week period—coming through different people and/or from different circumstances—I felt an important truth was being revealed in this serendipitous fashion. On these occasions, I felt I was being shown a veritable truth—first from one perspective, and then from another, until I finally understood the message.

Sometimes answers came almost immediately, or at the end of the day, after a good night's sleep, or even a week or so later. If I felt confused and prayed for peace and clarity I often experienced an immediate sense of peace, with clarity not far behind. If I felt mentally, emotionally, or physically distressed, the answer might first come as a gentle assurance in my mind and heart that, even in the midst of my pain, God was in charge and all was well. A gradual healing might follow over the next few days, weeks or months. Answers also came through dreams or out of meditation.

Early on, when answers weren't forthcoming right away, I realized the problem was not with God but with either my inability to see the answer right in front of me—or that I had not fully "let go and let God." I was now convinced that Spirit always hears and responds to our prayers, healing us on many levels. Sometimes I could sense and feel a subtle mental and emotional healing taking place right away. However, working at a molecular level far below my conscious awareness, a physical healing might take days, weeks, or months to show forth.

* * *

I was duly impressed to see a prayer box in the foyer on my first visit to the Science of Mind church. Obviously, these people believed in the healing power of prayer. Never having seen prayer offered to individuals in this manner, I wondered why traditional churches didn't offer such a service. The prayer box was brought forward at the close of each service and given to the minister, who then gave thanks that these prayers were already being answered. The box was then taken to the Ministry of Prayer room where each prayer request received special attention. Religious Science practitioners would speak the truth of God's healing presence and power for each one. I was curious to know more about this service.

Most every Sunday I filled out requests for my sister, Judy, and for myself, or whenever I found myself worrying about a friend or family member. Just knowing people were praying on our behalf helped ease some of my anxieties. Ernest Holmes wrote, "There is a power for good in the universe greater than we are, and we can use it." At first I didn't understand what that power was, but soon discovered he was talking about the healing power of prayer—the power of God working through our words of truth, spoken in faith, believing. Holmes renamed prayer "spiritual mind treatment," because he realized it wasn't so much that we needed to pray for God to hear and give us what we longed for, but rather to treat our own minds to recognize a higher truth, *for God already knows what we need but must wait for us to ask.* The truth is that God stands in our midst, awaiting our recognition, our asking, and our accepting of these gifts. In this new context, we can believe the truth that "it really is the Father's good pleasure to give us the kingdom," *(Luke 12:32)*

Spiritual mind treatments sounded quite different from the kind of prayer heard in traditional churches. They began as affirmations of the truth that God was/is the Creator and Sustainer of all life—All-loving, All-wise, All-powerful, and Everywhere Present. This description of God as an ever-present reality validated again my personal experience. I first noticed that spiritual mind treatments had an immediate relaxing, calming effect on my mind—something that my earlier prayers had never been able to elicit. These treatments were, in fact, both a mental and spiritual exercise—mental, because the work was taking place in my own mind, from my own thoughts, words and beliefs, and from my perception of truth—and spiritual, because in whatever circumstance I was immersed in, I understood that, from my human ego, I could do nothing. Even Jesus said, "It is not I, but the Father within who doeth the work."

Using "The Lord's Prayer" as one example, Dr. Holmes carefully analyzed the distinctive elements of this prayer and discovered five essential steps. Those five steps were: *Recognition, Unification, Realization, Thanksgiving, and Release:*

Recognition of God as Creator of the universe—of our life and all life;

Unification or identification with God as the source and substance of our life and/or the life of the one for whom we are praying;

Realization that the gifts of Spirit have already been given but must wait our asking and accepting; understanding that God gives us the freedom to say what it is we need and desire. At the same time, we must open and accept the good we seek. Above all, we are to believe that God, our Maker, truly loves us and desires our highest and greatest good, despite our shortcomings.

Thanksgiving is a sincere feeling of appreciation for life and all its blessings, and gratitude for God's promise of life, abundant.

Release: We must truly let go and allow Spirit to work its perfect work in and through us—or in the one for whom we are praying—trusting both the Love and the Law of God to know what to do, how to do, and when to do.

* * *

Over the centuries, of course, millions of people have prayed successfully without consciously following a set formula; yet these essential elements, however subtle, were in place. For a novice, just learning the art and science of prayer, I appreciated these guidelines. Working with this formula, step-by-step, my mind and heart were brought into alignment with Spirit. For me that first step—to recognize God as the Creator of all life wasn't difficult, but the next step of identifying and unifying with my Creator was. Intellectually, I could accept this truth, but my inability to rise above the mind-set of "unworthy sinner" to that of "the beloved" presented a block. To establish a true relationship with Spirit, I knew I must work through this issue. The realization step—knowing the gifts of Spirit waits my asking—seemed relatively easy. Giving thanks was the easiest of all, naturally feeling a deep sense of appreciation and gratitude for the generosity and blessings of Spirit.

The last step—release—was the hardest of all. Often thinking I had let go, I would find myself again fretting and nursing the problem. I now understood that my healing could not come until I fully gave it over to Spirit, until I could mentally and emotionally detach and trust the divine process. Using the analogy of writing a letter, I saw that if I didn't mail it, it would never arrive at its destination. The same was true for prayer/treatment. When I could fully and finally release the treatment, there was a response and a healing. "Let go and let God" became the by-word.

Spiritual Mind Treatments can be brief or lengthy, depending on how long it takes to reason out the truth of your convictions and meet those five steps. As a reader, you can use the following prototype as a guide to writing your own Spiritual Mind Treatment. Come from your heart, keep it simple, and in your own words define your situation, or the situation of the person you are praying for) as clearly as possible.

<u>Sample Spiritual Mind Treatment (for someone else):</u>

"There is only One life, One intelligence, One true power in the universe;

All Knowing, All Powerful, and Everywhere Present; God, Creator of the universe: Ultimate Intelligence, Infinite and Ineffable, from which all things come and to which all things return.

All that I am, all that (name) is, is some part of this one Life. I seek now to come into a greater realization of the oneness, the goodness, the presence and power of Spirit moving in, through, and over all life; in the life of (name) and in my life right here and right now.

I know that with God, all things are possible. Accepting as truth, that God has good for all of us, even beyond our ability to conceive, I ask for my friend, (name), the perfect res-

olution to her present difficulty, for mental clarity and direction, and for faith and courage to take action if needed.
With joy and gratitude I accept for her, and with her, all that she needs and desires to manifest her highest good right now—under grace and in perfect ways.
I now fully release these words into the love and law of divine Mind, from which all blessings flow.
In the name of this Christ Presence, I let it be so, and so it is! Amen."

* * *

In those early days I sometimes needed additional spiritual support. Fortunately, I could call on one of the licensed Religious Science practitioners in our church. Having someone I could trust to know the truth and speak it for me took a tremendous burden off my shoulders.

Before 1972 and my awakening, when presented with a problem that seemed to have no solution, did I think to pray for guidance and direction? Finding myself in a situation that had become untenable, did I call for help? Were most people like me—resistant to prayer even in times of crisis? By the same token, did those who believed in prayer pray regularly, and were they getting positive results? St. Paul encouraged his followers to pray without ceasing; meaning, I think, to keep a positive word of truth continually activated in their minds. While this is what I wanted, negative influences constantly fought for my attention.

Paul refers to this condition—of knowing and affirming the truth and, at the same time, not always being able to act on that truth. This appears to be one of life's many paradoxes. Seeking to live our lives from our conscious reasoning mind, we are often unaware of the subtle influences, negative and positive, coming to us from the world around us and from our own subconscious minds. A way, a method, is needed by which we can stay tuned to the deeper truth of God's caring Presence. Spiritual Mind Treatments became that method for me.

* * *

In earlier days, when my attention was scattered among myriad activities and interests, I couldn't imagine my thoughts, words and beliefs having the power to create much of anything—good or bad. Once I understood that my words had the power to heal or harm, I knew I was responsible for the ways in which I used them. Why, I wondered, have we been kept in the dark about our active, but unconscious, participation in this creative process? Our power to bless or curse another is still largely unrecognized by the masses—perhaps for good reason. Maybe it's far better to be ignorant of this latent power than to develop and knowingly misuse it.

Learning to pray 'correctly' has become an important part of my life for this reason—when my mind is in league with the Mind of God, when my heart is centered in divine love— miracles happen even in the midst of chaos. Prayer is learning to ask and accept the good God has for us, knowing that our good doesn't take away from someone else's good. Prayer, for me, is a continuous exercise in surrendering my limited human understanding to the Divine Will. My primary goal is to think good, not evil; love, not hate; peace, not confusion; praise, not condemnation. Prayer is a source of strength and nourishment that helps keep me on the spiritual path and in "the divine flow."

When in doubt and needing to convince myself of the truth I am affirming, my prayers can sometimes be quite lengthy. Other times, when I want a reminder of a simple truth, short affirmations are sufficient. Both are part of my prayer life. Our prayers can take other forms as well; coming from a loving, compassionate heart as a simple word of encouragement, even a gentle smile to a stranger, or a reassuring touch. For the power of our creative mind to be a true blessing to the world, it must be administered under the aegis of divine love and wisdom. Anything less means we are operating from our human ego, which has its own agenda.

In Phil. 4:18, St. Paul gives a beautiful definition of prayer: "...Whatsoever things are true, whatsoever things are honest, whatsoever things are just, whatsoever things are pure, whatsoever things are lovely, whatsoever things are of good report; if there be any virtue, and if there be any praise, think on these things." Affirming the good, the true and the beautiful has always brought me into a consciousness of my oneness with Spirit.

Chapter 9

"And seek not ye what ye shall eat, or what ye shall drink, neither be ye of doubtful mind. For all these things do the nations of the world seek after: and your Father knoweth that ye have need of these things, But rather seek ye the kingdom of God; and all these things shall be added unto you."
Luke 12: 29, 31

As you now know, when I became involved in spiritual studies in the early 70's I was dealing with the onset of rheumatoid arthritis—experiencing some pain, fever, and growing stiffness in my joints. Surprisingly, my first priority was not about a physical healing, although it was a close second. Certainly I needed some understanding of how to best care for my physical body. After all, rheumatoid arthritis supposedly had no cure. This dose of reality forced me to face three awful truths:

1) Doctors weren't infallible after all. (I had so hoped they were.)

2) There was no one in the medical field who could "fix" me.

3) Ultimately, I realized that life comes as a Do-It-Yourself Kit.

Hoping there *might* be a cure out there somewhere if I could just find it, I looked in the direction of alternative therapies. Many new (to the western world) healing techniques were just coming into vogue—acupuncture being one example. Health magazines, books on healing, and health food stores were sprouting up everywhere. Although I doubted the right diet and the right mix of vitamin and minerals could cure me, they might enhance the quality of my life. Besides, what other options were there?

Was there a right diet—a right formula? Unfortunately, I knew no one knowledgeable in this field. More or less on my own, I hoped to educate myself by reading books on nutrition, vitamin, and mineral supplements, and researching alternative therapies. Before long, this information began to blur. One book touted raw milk as the answer, not only for rheumatoid arthritis, but also for many other illnesses. Several months later, I read another book claiming all milk products should be eliminated from an arthritic's diet. Numerous contradictions like these abounded. Also, conditioned to the immediate benefits of drugs, I hadn't realized vitamin therapy and other healing modalities take much longer to effect a change.

Neither trusting my ability to intuit the right regimen for myself nor believing in the efficacy of most of these products, I experimented with first one and then another. Nothing appeared to work. Before I knew what had happened, I had developed a full-blown ulcer. It could have been a side effect from my prescribed pain medication, but certainly helping it along was my growing anxiety and frustration over not having a true direction and course of action. In hindsight, with my limited knowledge, attempting to sort out what to do was foolish. As I asked for divine guidance and understanding, these words of Jesus kept coming to mind: "Seek not what ye shall eat or drink, for your Father knows what you have need of, but seek ye first the kingdom of God, and all these things shall be given unto you."

I hardly knew what to make of it. Jesus, most likely, was speaking to people who had little to eat or drink and who perhaps wondered where their next meal was coming from. In my case, I hoped for a cure from the right diet. As for "seeking first the kingdom," I thought that was what I was doing in my studies. This Science of Mind philosophy was not only a mental science; it was also a spiritual psychology, providing ways and means to live a spiritual life. No doubt, Spirit meant this message, "Seek first the kingdom," to lead me out of my anxieties and fears back into the 'Light.'

By 1973, my outer life appeared calm, belying the inner chaos. At the time, I was serving a second two-year term on the National Board of the Kiwi Club, an organization of former American Airlines stewardesses. A member of local chapters for fifteen years, I briefly considered running for national president the following year, but then realized too much was happening in my inner life to consider such a move. Still deeply worried over my young sister's illness, I had now added the burden of searching for a magic cure. In the meantime, the arthritis was still active and beginning to limit some of my activities.

Contemplating again this statement, "seek first the kingdom...," I turned to Scripture for clarity of what we are meant to seek. I found the following verses:

> "Therefore I say unto you, Take no thought for your life, what ye shall eat, neither for the body, what ye shall put on. The life is more than meat, and the body more than raiment...Consider the ravens; for they neither sow nor reap, which neither have storehouse nor barn; and God feedeth them; how much more are ye better than the fowls? And which of you with taking thought can add to his stature one cubit? If ye then be not able to do that thing which is least, why take ye thought for the rest? (Luke 12: 22-25)
>
> "Consider the lilies of the field, how they grow, they toil not, neither do they spin; and yet I say unto you, that even Solomon in all his glory was not arrayed like one of these. If then God so clothe the grass, which is today in the field and tomorrow is cast into the oven; how much more will he clothe you, O ye of little faith? (Luke 12: 27,28)
>
> "And seek not ye what ye shall eat, or what ye shall drink, neither be ye of doubtful mind. For all these things do the nations of the world seek after; and your Father knoweth that ye have need of these things. But rather seek ye the kingdom of God; and all these things shall be added unto you...Fear not, little flock, for it is your Father's good pleasure to give you the kingdom." (Luke 12: 29-32)

In these verses, Jesus appears to be speaking of a holy Presence within that knows what we need and will guide us once we let go our doubts and fears and begin to trust its leadings. Gradually I began to see that, while we are to do what we know to do, we are not to fret or worry or become anxious when we do not know what to do. More and more, I realized this was my problem. Overwhelmed by this disease, my problem was my inability to let go mentally and emotionally and trust the Indwelling Presence.

Some time during this period a most amazing incident occurred in a personal growth workshop at our Science of Mind church. I had asked for the group's prayers regarding a growing fear of becoming an invalid. I had watched in horror as Lupus, an immune disease similar to rheumatoid arthritis, severely deformed my young sister's hands. Sometime during our silent prayers, I began to feel a subtle sensation in my chest cavity, and in awe, witnessed a grayish wispy vapor emerge from my chest. Having come up and out of my body, this misty cloud hovered for some seconds around my upper chest—and then around my head—before finally dissipating. Never having experienced anything of this nature before, I was spell-bound.

This was *not* a physical experience, but rather a psycho/spiritual phenomenon of some kind. I realized that what I was sensing was invisible to others in the group. Having trusted this group to speak on my behalf, my deepest fears of becoming crippled by this disease had been released in a most unusual fashion. Who would have believed that Spirit would respond to my request in such a dramatic and powerful way? Since that experience, the thought of being crippled has not been of further concern to me.

My idea of what had actually risen up out of my chest was based on something I had read in the past about crystallized thought-forms—what they were, and how they become crystallized. My understanding was that the thoughts that hold us in bondage, either through our fear or fascination, can eventually become crystallized or hardened in our psyche. Like our core beliefs, they hunker down and make themselves invisible within the body/mind/psyche. Whatever this "crystallized thought-form," was, it seems to have shattered and broken apart as a result of our prayers, releasing the dispersed energy as a misty vapor. Thanks to this loving group of people, I was healed in a most unusual and profound way.

* * *

As time moved forward, I continued to seek out alternative healing methods; still unsure which ones were authentic. What I needed was another sign! A few days later a fellow student from my Science of Mind class called. Having a problem with her eyes, she asked if I could drive her to her chiropractor /acupuncturist. Of course, I was glad to oblige. However, the flags went up in my "conditioned" mind about the credibility of chiropractic and acupuncture practices. Were these therapies effective?

My resistance seemed counter to what I was trying to accomplish. Perhaps here was an opportunity to overcome my doubts—and trust "guidance." As I thumbed through some magazines in the waiting room, I thought that maybe, just maybe, this man could help me. Reluctant to ask, I prayed about it and then thought, *"If the opportunity presents itself and feels right, I will speak to him."*

The procedure of acupuncture calls for inserting needles and leaving them for a certain length of time. Because there were no other patients requiring the doctor's attention he came into the waiting room and sat down to chat. His son had just gone into the navy and I told him I had a son at West Point. The conversation continued in this vein—of family, the weather, and local news. Then, without making a conscious decision to do so, I asked him if he thought acupuncture could help me. He felt it could and, subsequently, I began a series of chiropractic adjustments and acupuncture treatments in all of my affected joints.

My body/mind system had been stagnant for so long and the swelling and inflammation in all of my joints so severe that I was surprised to feel a subtle response from those beginning treatments. It felt like my body was saying, "At last she's taking some action!" Putting aside my ego-controlling mind to allow a greater good in the form of this doctor's expertise was a *big, big* step for me. After three months of weekly treatments, there was a huge difference in the way I felt and moved.

As for what I should eat or drink in order to be healed of this disease, I found no magic formula waiting my discovery in yet another book. What I did find, when I remembered to ask, were these Bible verses counseling me to cease worrying about a perfect diet; place myself under divine authority, and trust its wisdom. This action was effective in lifting my errant mind out of the slough of so many contradictory theories and regimens on health, bringing my mind and heart to focus on God as my Ever-Present Guidance System. Soon thereafter came a flash of insight into the power and value of simple mealtime blessings—an instant reminder that, indeed, our food is blessed.

Grudgingly at first, then step by step, I began to edge past my conscious mind to listen to inner guidance and counsel. I slowly realized that my strong resistance had separated me not only from my good but from divine guidance as well. Despite having been once held in the loving Light of God, I was not able to reenter this inner world from my ego-state-of-mind. Despite a beginning intellectual understanding of universal laws and principles—despite growing evidence that, through spiritual mind treatments, I was being healed in many ways—the deeper experience of 'practicing the Presence' eluded me. How was I to proceed?

I wanted to experience and feel these truths in my inner being, to embody these truths, and to make them an integral part of my being. Dr. Holmes spoke of the embodiment of truth as essential. Dr. Amos referred to it as "the mystical marriage of the head and the heart." Perhaps the only way to "marry" the head and the heart was through quiet contemplation, through the practice of silent meditation—a practice I decided to pursue.

Chapter 10

"I will lift up mine eyes unto the hills
from whence cometh my help."
Psalm 121:1

My next realization was the need to take dominion over my mind and emotions. This was the decade of the '70s when Transcendental Meditation was popular. Using a Sanskrit word as a mantra felt too foreign to me, so I decided to learn on my own from the many "How to meditate" books on the market.

To my knowledge, meditation wasn't touted or widely practiced in the Christian faith, except in monasteries. In my own church experience, I had never heard anyone mention meditation as a viable spiritual practice. Considered an eastern religious practice and, therefore, initially suspect to my conditioned mind, the idea nevertheless had presented itself and I decided to follow the lead.

Remembering Dr. Holmes' admonition to always enter prayer and meditation holding in mind our very highest concept of God, I began. This reminder not only helped hold my focus and intention; I felt it was also a protection from other forces in the psyche. Having bought several books on meditation I diligently began the prescribed procedure. "Breathe deeply and slowly; focus your mind's eye on a single idea, word, phrase, or object; find a time and a place where you will not be disturbed or distracted; begin to make this a daily practice." Setting a time and place, I began the deep breathing exercises, trying to relax my body, quiet my mind, and calm my emotions.

What a lesson in self-discovery! I was amazed at how difficult it was to truly relax my body and quiet my thoughts. The breathing exercises helped. Entering meditation for the first time, I became aware of myself as an observer, getting a look, as if over my shoulder, at thoughts flitting across the screen of my mind—much like a video, except mine seemed to be on fast-forward! My mind was all over the place, jumping around like a 'hyper–activated' monkey. Bringing these thoughts and feelings under control was going to take some doing. Nonetheless, I resolved to stay with it, remembering another of Jesus' statements, "The light of the body is the eye; if therefore thine eye be single, thy whole body shall be full of light." (Matt.6:22)

Surprised by how many extraneous thoughts fought for my attention, I couldn't get my mind to hold a single idea for any length of time. (I later learned this is a common problem for beginners.) Repeating a single word or phrase, such as "Peace" or "God is Love," was definitely not working. After numerous unsuccessful attempts, I decided to just sit quietly and concentrate on something familiar. I chose "The Twenty-Third Psalm." I had always loved this poem, having once known it by heart, and it came back to memory easily.

Focusing on just one or two phrases at a time—moving slowly and methodically, it took weeks to go through the entire psalm. Taking one phrase at a time, I repeated the words over and over, aloud and silently, until at one point they seemed to drop into a deeper place within my psyche. Every line of this great psalm was like a healing balm. Actually, working through the entire psalm took six months for me to realize the extent of the healing. It took that long to relax the twitches in both eyes. This recognition made me aware of two important facts—the power of this healing Psalm as a meditation, and the condition of my nervous system.

Breathing deeply, and pausing often between phrases, I began:

The Lord is my Shepherd.....the Lord is my Shepherd.....the Lord is my Shepherd........

I shall not want.....I shall not want......(breathing deeply)

I shall not want ......I shall not want..........

He maketh me to lie down in green pastures.........He maketh me to lie down in green pastures.......He maketh me to lie down.........(breathing deeply—moving slowly.)

He leadeth me beside the still waters.........He leadeth me beside the still waters............

He restoreth my soul..............He restoreth my soul...........He restoreth my soul........

He leadeth me in paths of righteousness, for his name's sake............He leadeth me in paths of righteousness...........He leadeth me in paths.........

Yea, though I walk through the valley of the shadow of death, I will fear no evil....... Yea, though I walk through the valley of the shadow of death, I will fear no evil....... for Thou art with me.........for Thou art with me......for Thou art with me.....

Thy rod and Thy staff they comfort me......Thy rod and Thy staff they comfort me.....

Thou preparest a table before me in the presence of mine enemies ......Thou anointest my head with oil. .....

My cup runneth over......

Surely goodness and mercy shall follow me all the days of my life......

and I will dwell in the house of the Lord forever.

This wonderful psalm finally quieted, calmed, and healed my mind. Another meditation mantra that worked well for me is the title of this chapter, "I will lift up mine eyes unto the hills, from whence cometh my help." These words seemed to actually lift and focus my inner eye on spiritual truth, taking me into a deeper silence. Over the years, I have found other powerful statements to use as mantras, committing many to memory to repeat in quiet moments.

The following verses were also assurances that when we turn our thoughts to God we find comfort in his Presence.

"He that dwelleth in the secret place of the Most High shall abide under the shadow of the Almighty." Psalms 91:1

"Because thou hast made the Lord, which is your refuge, even the Most High, thy habitation, there shall no evil befall thee, neither shall any plague come nigh thy dwelling. For He shall give His angels charge over thee, to keep thee in all thy ways." Psalms 91:9-11

* * *

Some people, having learned to meditate more formally, might think my first efforts were not true meditation, yet they served me well. They brought me important insights into a part of my nature that could only be accessed through this method of quiet contemplation. Meditation gave me a good look at the state of my inner life and its need for healing. In this endeavor to quiet my mind, I discovered I was a "head person," meaning I was more comfortable analyzing and figuring things out than getting in touch with my intuitive feeling nature. Not having known that my intuition was my connection to Spirit, I had not only devalued its worth, but had distrusted its wisdom as well. Instead, I had made a god of the ego/intellect, valuing it as primary. Out of touch with my deepest feelings, I had lost something vital and necessary to my health and well-being.

One insight that surprised me came when I awakened one day to the lack of joy in my soul. When had life gotten so heavy and serious? It was as though God heard my concern. Shortly after, the following poem on an artist friend's wall, done in calligraphy and decorated with little pink flowers and black butterflies, caught my eye. It said, "God respects me when I work. He loves me when I sing." I used to sing. When did I stop and why? While meditating on joy one day, suddenly I saw myself sitting on a fluffy white cloud—a transparent little spirit. My feelings of lightness and joy were so exhilarating I felt like I might fly away at any moment. Then appearing next to me was a little clothespin with which to anchor myself to the cloud! Paradoxically, as I opened to joy I also opened to places of sadness as the following verses reveal.

Alone

For the first time in my life, I find myself alone and I am shocked at the strong emotions coming forth!

I feel an overwhelming sense of fear, mixed with sadness, and a sudden realization that in truth one ultimately must walk through life—and death—alone.

No one can be with me through all of life's experiences to give me strength and support. Somehow I must find these resources within myself.

Aware of how it is and how it has to be, I begin to cultivate a joy in aloneness, and with it, a greater sense of peace and serenity.

In prayer and meditation I find a solitary strength as I listen for that still, small voice.
It establishes me in my soul with God, my Source, and with all life.

It's not too late

If I had only known the present,
acknowledged just some of
my many blessings,
been aware of sights and
sounds and light and color,
attuned to music, to silence,
to my own inner harmony—

But I was numb, somehow blinded,
my senses caught in human play,
my dreams a million miles away.
I couldn't see the joy all 'round me—
nor within me. Somehow along
the way, I had lost touch with magic
and wonder.

Now—even though the years have gone
when youth and all that means has
passed; Asleep and now awake,
I see a new beginning, I feel an
unfamiliar sense of joy and sparkle—
And I know it's not too late.

These verses were written some time in the mid-80's, revealing my past and present state of affairs, yet with words of hope and promise—and joy.

Not long after I began the practice of meditation, three related visions came to me over a period of a month. I had not had any significant dreams since the vision of the river and the mountain. (Actually, visions have been rare in my meditation experience, but the few I've had have been profound.)

The Three Visions:

> In the first scene, I was standing in front of an old nondescript house. The landscape was gray with dusty overtones. On my right, further away, was a long wooden building resembling a warehouse, with a tin roof and loading platform. I saw no people or signs of life anywhere. To my left on a high rise above me was a beautiful, white walled city. The walls were so high all I could see above them were the tops of palm trees glistening green in the sunlight.
> The city looked inviting and I must have been thinking of approaching it when unexpectedly an angel carrying a lute appeared beside the wall. She was so tall the top of the city wall came only to her waist. The lute she was carrying might as well have been a machine gun as far as I was concerned. The message was clear—the city was off-limits!
>
> A week or so later a following sequence to that dream:
> I was standing under a tree just inside the gate of this walled city, observing a large gathering of women and children around a central fountain where a man, who I took to be Jesus, was talking. There was much joy and laughter among the crowd. As I watched from a distance, this man, who I assumed was Jesus, looked up, caught, and held my eye for a moment, and smiled.

> Several weeks passed before the third and final sequence: Now I was standing at the fountain facing the man I had seen in my previous dreams. Again he smiled a warm smile and offered me a cup of water, which I took and drank.
>
> Later I remembered something Jesus was reported to have said to the woman at the well about living waters. ". . . whosoever drinketh of the water that I shall give him shall never thirst, but the water that I shall give him, shall be in him a well of water springing up into everlasting life." (John 4:14)

These visions/dreams were a startling revelation to me of the condition of my soul and my current place on the spiritual path. There was much to ponder in these three visions. At least they seemed to indicate progress. Had the rejection of the 'hellfire and damnation' part of my religion effectively separated me from the positive aspects as well? Then another memory floated into my mind: The day my friends and I joined the church, I wasn't sure of my commitment. I wanted to marry and have a family. I did not want to be a missionary in a foreign land, which I must have thought was Jesus' plan for my life. Had these thoughts and feelings, in some significant way, separated me further from my faith and belief in him?

I was sure these visions, with their amazing insights into my past, were a result of meditation. Silence provided a place to sense that inner spiritual reality—to attune and listen for that still, small voice. In the quietness of meditation I found a place that allowed me to redeem myself and to make friends, not only with Jesus, but also with unknown parts of myself. By focusing my mind's eye on a single ray of "light" I was open to deeper realizations of Truth, of God, and of who I was as a spiritual being.

Meditation is the bridge that has allowed me to safely cross the river in my first prophetic dream, and to move toward my journey up the mountain! I owe much to those images of Jesus that have reappeared to guide me along the path. Both prayer and meditation have been keys to healing the rift within my soul, bringing me back to center—and to God, my Source. I discovered silence to be—not an end in and of itself—but rather an opening to greater resources that lie within. The discipline of meditation has been difficult—taking persistence, patience, and a dedication I didn't know I had—but the benefits have been priceless.

Chapter 11

"If ye continue in my word,
then are ye my disciples indeed."
John 8:31

If I had been told when I began my Science of Mind studies in 1973 that I would continue through all the requirements and become licensed as a professional practitioner, I would not have believed it. My original goal was to find greater spiritual understanding and a healing of mind, body, and spirit; however, over time the idea of becoming a practitioner emerged. It seemed a logical transition to move into the public arena at some point—to serve others as I was being served. Certainly this was a profession of high calling and dedication; perhaps this was the career for which I'd been searching.

In my beginning classes, while some abstract principles were difficult to grasp and impossible to articulate, they were, nonetheless, deeply satisfying to my soul. Incorporating these principles into my life, my faith in the power of prayer and the truth of these principles was firmly established. With a change in my attitude, I noticed subtle healings within my family and in myself. As far as I was concerned, learning, step by step, how to live in harmony with God, with others, and with myself through right thinking, right speaking, and right believing (which is a Buddhist teaching), was also *applied* Christianity.

I felt blessed to have found, in the study of the Science of Mind philosophy, universal principles to help explain the mysteries of the Bible. These new studies gave substance, purpose, and direction for my life. Over the years, my teachers have been many: I was introduced to Phineas Parkhurst Quimby as the father of the New Thought Movement. Denominations born out of the healing principles he discovered and practiced in the 1860's include Christian Science, Religious Science, Divine Science, and Unity, and perhaps others.

Although my spiritual education began as a child with the New Testament teachings of Jesus, it was Ernest Holmes' book, *The Science of Mind,* that helped clarify the depth of those teachings. For example; I had not comprehended the deeper meaning and import of one of Jesus' well-known verses, "I have come that ye might have life and have it more abundantly." Although I believed this statement was fundamentally true, I had not thought of the abundant life in earthly terms; only in terms of the after-life. Here was a broader view—that God has also given us the resources to live the abundant life here and now. As humans, the dilemma we face is that we do not understand that God, as the love and the law of our lives, must wait in silence, unseen and unfelt, for us to make our request.

In my disbelief, I had failed to see my connection to God, the source and supply of my every good. I had forgotten, *if I ever knew,* that God has good for me *right now* beyond my wildest imaginings. I had not known that my good must await my asking. Understanding that God's good is limitless and all-encompassing, and that my good does not take away from someone else's good, was a monumental revelation. And so I began to ask for whatever I needed in any given moment—whether it was for strength and power to persevere in adversity, for courage to face my fears, for patience, compassion, or for forgiveness. Knowing that God was my source of abundant good—I knew that *if this was true for me, it was true for all.*

This and all other spiritual principles rooted in Scripture were anything but new, but for me they had remained veiled and hidden until my eyes were opened. As I learned more about God as the abundant life, I naturally wanted to share these ideas with others—but that wasn't possible except to those open to such ideas. Not many were. Sadly, the truth that God wants good for us far beyond what we can conceive and believe remains practically unknown to the masses. I thought of at least three reasons why we do not experience the fullness of God's abundant love: our skepticism, an ingrained belief that we are unworthy of God's abundance, and a failure to ask God to bless and prosper us in ways beyond our conscious knowing.

As indicated earlier, the idea that God could straighten out the crooked places in my life was beyond me. From the western mind-set I inherited I found it hard to believe in anything that couldn't be scientifically reproduced and measured in laboratory experiments. But that was before my "Light/Energy" experience. Now that I had a different orientation, I believed and accepted God as The Living Spirit Almighty, the Creator of all there is, as the Life undergirding my life, and all life. Although unable to fathom the power of God, measure the activity of Spirit, or the healing power of a love, transcendent; nonetheless, I knew that such things were real.

Even though my studies brought new understanding of God, of Jesus, the man; Jesus, the Christ; and the indwelling Presence, I faced paradoxes at every turn. I could see good, but I could also see evil. I could accept this higher Truth, this Absolute Reality of Only One Life—God, the Good Omnipotent, existing on the invisible side of life—but I could see as well that we humans are held in the thrall of a world view that believes *more* in the power of evil *over* us than in the power of God working *for* us. As a result, the law of—it is "done unto us as we believe" has become our lot.

Today we are living in a new age, when global events and circumstances demand answers beyond our capacity to solve. A heightened awareness of God's availability and willingness to come to our collective aid is sorely needed. I wonder if we could demonstrate enough faith to orchestrate, for even one day, a worldwide event where peoples of all nations could declare in unison the greater power of God to overcome our collective belief in the power of evil. What might happen? Even more mind-boggling, if we could hold a realization of God as the Ultimate Power, long enough and strong enough—could our collective faith bring the world back into harmony and balance? Could such endeavors be enough to overcome our collective belief in evil and, quite possibly, alter the course of human history? With the faith of millions I believed it could! These were my thoughts as I processed this teaching of God as All There Is—an Ineffable Power and Presence—standing in the midst of what we label "good" and "evil."

The book, *Satan is Alive and Well on Planet Earth,* became a best seller in 1972. After my experience of the holy Presence, I felt that someone needed to write a rebuttal and title it, *Spirit is Alive and*

Well on Planet Earth." Everyone already believes in evil as a presence in the world, did we need to further prove the point? I pondered the question of why, as a human species, we are so fascinated with evil, to the point where we want it graphically displayed in magazines, tabloids, books, and on our television, movie, and computer screens. What is it that attracts us? Is the play of good and evil the perennial struggle of the human soul? After all, the pull of opposites does create a certain kind of excitement, without which life might appear exceedingly dull. Is it perhaps that we develop our spiritual muscles and learn our soul's lessons through this play of opposites within ourselves?

Certainly, evil seems real to us when we witness first hand, or on the nightly news, 'man's inhumanity to man.' We know those feelings to be strong and, at times, almost overpowering, when our own emotions of anger and rage erupt. In those moments we catch a glimpse of what evil would look like if we allowed our rage to fully vent. On the other hand, our inner goodness works in silence—quietly, gently, and subtly. This good often goes unnoticed and unappreciated simply because we are unaware of good as a force and a power—greater than evil—within us. The following excerpts provide a window into the beliefs of my early teachers and how they influenced my understanding of truth.

Dr. Holmes, speaking of spiritual mind treatment in his book, *The Science of Mind*:

> Treatment is not *willing* things to happen; it is to provide within ourselves an avenue through which they may happen. Treatment opens up the avenues of thought, expands the consciousness, and lets Reality through; it clarifies the mentality, removes the obstruction of thought and lets in the Light; it removes doubt and fear, in the realization of the Presence of Spirit, and is necessary while we are confronted by obstructions or obstacles. We already live in a Perfect Universe, but (this Universe) needs to be seen mentally before it can become a part of our experience. Every problem is primarily mental, and the answer to all problems will be found in Spiritual Realization.

Ralph Waldo Emerson, in his essay, *The Oversoul*:

From within or from behind, a light shines through us upon things and makes us aware that we are nothing, but the light is all. And from his essay, *Spiritual Laws*: "There is a soul at the centre of nature and over the will of every man, so that none of us can wrong the universe. It has so infused its strong enchantment into nature that we prosper when we accept its advice, and when we struggle to wound its creatures our hands are glued to our sides, or they beat our own breasts. The whole course of things goes to teach us faith. We need only obey. There is a guidance for each of us, and by lowly listening we shall hear the right word.

From Judge Thomas Troward's, *The Edinburgh Lectures on Mental Science*: (Troward was a Scotsman who, through meditation and the study of the Scriptures, wrote and lectured widely in Scotland in the 1920s.)

The principle of growth is that of inherent vitality in the seed itself, and the operations of the gardener have their exact analogue in Mental Science. We do not put the self-expansive vitality into the seed, but we must sow it, and we may also, so to speak, water it by quiet concentrated contemplation of our desire as an actually accomplished fact. But we must carefully remove from such contemplation any idea of a strenuous effort on our part to *make* the seed grow....such contemplation should be accompanied by a feeling of pleasure and restfulness in foreseeing the certain accomplishment of our desires. This is making our requests known to God *with thanksgiving* which St. Paul recommends.

Emma Curtis Hopkins was considered the "teacher of teachers" among her peers and her students, because she taught most, if not all, the leaders and founders in the New Thought Movement. She was eighty years old when she began to instruct Ernest Holmes in 1924, imparting to him the element of mysticism that, according to his brother,

Fenwicke, Ernest had felt was missing in his teaching. From her book, Scientific Christian Mental Practice: she says:

God is Spirit, therefore it is the Science of Spirit which we are to study when we open the reasoning with the word 'God.' God is the name for that Intelligence which out of its own substance bestowed upon you that intelligence you now have. Intelligence is Mind...By Mind alone we are taught to live and be strong. By Mind alone we are supported and defended. Jesus said, "Man shall not live by bread alone, but by every word that proceedeth out of the mouth of God.

She goes on to say that "Everybody, nearly, tries to cover up the main purpose of his life. He tells all kinds of stories to himself and others about what he is seeking. Often he tells that all he asks is just enough to feed and clothe and house his family. Let him tell the honest truth—that he seeks for unlimited bounty. The unconscious truth is that there is Good for us and we ought to have it. Nothing can kill that unconscious feeling. It is indestructible. It is omnipotent.

In all thy ways acknowledge Him and He will direct thy paths. To acknowledge God is to admit we are seeking our good...It is well to give one day a week to acknowledging that we are seeking our good. We say what our Good is. It is freedom, peace, joy, fulfillment, a sense of well-being, strength, confidence, harmony, order, balance, a sense of abundant good in every area of our life—in our inner self, in our relationships, in our business and in our financial affairs.

Mrs. Hopkins saw a unified instruction that runs almost verbatim through all the sacred books of the world. The way of salvation, as she saw it, was to get back to the basic truth by cutting through all the dogma of religion. From her book, *High Mysticism*:

> To look upward with the mystic eye is to start on the saving Tao. Look unto Me, and be ye saved—I will turn away your captivity from before your eyes when ye turn unto Me seeking My face, declared the two great prophets, Isaiah and Jeremiah…Lifting the inner eye to Him who is above reason, lights the two outer eyes to see the world in a new aspect, gives the tongue new descriptions of the world, and tips the pen with fadeless phrases…
>
> *For that thou seest, man,*
> *That too become thou must*
> *God if thou seest God,*
> *Dust if thou seest dust.*

From *The Quimby Manuscripts*: edited by Horatio Dresser; Introduction by Dr. Erwin Seale:

Quimby discovered that man has two levels of mind and that his thoughts are active in the upper level but his beliefs are active in the lower level and that these beliefs have a life and an authority of their own." He (Quimby) goes on to say, "I found that mind was something that could be changed, I called it *spiritual matter* because I found it could be condensed into a solid and receive a name called *tumor* and by the power, under a different direction, it might be dissolved and made to disappear.

He found the Bible word Christ to be synonymous with his term, the Scientific Man. He understood that the "individual mind that beholds the Scientific Man within itself is saved from its false beliefs and its troublesome experiences. And this Saviour is within every man.

Quimby saw that the mere repetition of what we nowadays call suggestions or affirmations was not enough. He saw too that the personal resources of any individual, however wonderful, however elevated and however knowledgeable, was not enough. The true healer must free himself from his false beliefs.

It was my understanding that Quimby healed Mary Baker Eddy and taught her the principles of science and health. Yet, there is some controversy between the Christian Science Church and the New Thought Movement as to the definitive role Quimby played in Eddy's life and teachings. On the basis of a personal healing, as well as her understanding of the spiritual principles Quimby taught, Mary Baker Eddy established the Christian Science church.

I've been asked on occasion if *Religious Science* is *Christian Science.* The answer is "No." There are similarities, but also differences. Both religions perceive God as a healing Presence that can be invoked through the prayers of those who believe in this Presence and power. Christian Science, as I understand it, holds that God can heal without benefit of outside medical help. I agree that this is quite possible for those who are able to *fully embody* this truth. Aware that people of faith can be healed through faith and prayer, Religious Science, nonetheless, accepts and appreciates medical knowledge and the healing arts because we recognize that all knowledge is God-given. At our present stage of development, most of us need the help of medicine and other healing modalities, and of course, the love of family and friends to support us in our healing.

Christian Science, I believe, confines itself to the study of two books—*The Holy Bible* and Mary Baker Eddy's *Science and Health.* Religious Science holds an open-ended view that truth can be found in every religion and in every sacred scripture; indeed, God is forever revealing more of his truth to those who have ears to hear. I believe professional practitioners in both Christian Science and Religious Science work from similar views of God as the Giver of all life.

I make this statement on the basis of an article I read many years ago while awaiting a flight home from Nashville. I noticed a Christian Science pamphlet on an empty seat nearby. A student practitioner had been given an assignment to see God, despite any appearance to the contrary, in the first person she encountered on her way home from class. A student practitioner myself at the time, I was fascinated by what I read. She told of walking across a city park and the first person she met was a derelict, a 'wino,' staggering in her direction. Her immediate reaction was to think, "How can I see God in this man?" She then realized he was expressing life, even if that expression looked limited and destructive. Her reasoning in truth was that God is the giver of life.

The divine seed was inherent in this man's life, in the innermost part of his being, waiting to be recognized and acknowledged. As he approached her she began to focus her attention on this divine truth. As he passed by, he smiled and said, "Thank you," muttering that he suddenly felt better. I wonder if the student/writer was as amazed and awed as I was reading her article—that her affirmation of God within this man had found an immediate response in him. That story was proof enough of the healing power of words of truth spoken for another human being.

Chapter 12

"...the words that I speak unto you
I speak not of myself: but the Father
that dwelleth in me, he doeth the works."
John 14:10

I was reminded often by my teachers that a practitioner works in the realm of mind only, with no sense of personal responsibility. Because the law is the doer, we were to trust this law completely. We were to work solely with statements of Truth, affirming God, as an Everywhere-present healing Reality. It was important to believe, accept, and affirm that every living being, every living thing, is a creation of the Divine, and because God called it good, we are compelled to call all of creation good as well. This intensive training was called *The Science of Mind*, but was actually a deeper understanding of Biblical truths. My commitment to these studies required a simple trust and an open mind.

Dr. Holmes said it well:

> The human mind needs, and must have, a direct approach to Spirit. It is natural for us to reach out from our ignorance to It's enlightenment, from our weakness to It's strength, from our darkness to It's light. Somewhere along the line we shall have to surrender our weakness to It's strength, our fear to It's faith, our lack to It's abundance.

> The practitioner of spiritual mind science must know that he/she is using a Law of cause and effect which is immutable. It knows how to do anything. It knows how to take (our) thoughts and ideas and actually project them into specific conditions. These conditions will automatically correspond to (our) mental acceptance, to (our) real, actual and embodied subjective acceptance and identification. (We) not only have a right to individualize creative power, nature has imposed this necessity upon (us.) (We have) no choice other than to use this creative power. (Our) thought will always be creative, whether (we) know it or not.

* * *

One of the paradoxes I encountered in the application of truth was the ease with which the mind could be lifted once a higher truth was acknowledged and affirmed, and how our old habitual beliefs keep returning, again and again. Once I understood the nature of my belief patterns to keep reappearing, I ceased blaming myself when they surfaced. Instead, I celebrated how quickly words of truth could dispel their power over me. Every time a belief came forward that was negative or limiting, if I addressed it *immediately* with a strong affirmation of truth, its power instantly vanished. However, when I allowed my emotions to get the upper hand, I became caught in my problem.

* * *

In 1976, having completed the required studies, I became a practitioner and a member of the Ministry of Prayer in the Tulsa Church. Routinely, whether I had appointments or not, my day began with prayer and meditation. I couldn't rest on the truth I already knew, or work I had done the previous day. The success of a practitioner, Dr. Holmes reminded us, hinged on the ability to separate the belief from the believer—first in the practitioner's mind and then in the mind of the client. This meant that before I could help others, I first had to separate myself from the same belief they were holding. Once this was accomplished, the client could experience healing on some level.

Before every appointment, I gave myself a thorough spiritual mind treatment, raising my consciousness to the truth of God, Omnipresent. My petition was to be a clear channel through which Divine love and wisdom could emerge and, as needed, the right word spoken. Emma Curtis Hopkins had said there is a "right word," and that word is different for every person, in every moment, and in every circumstance. It is the word needing to be spoken and needing to be heard.

Every time I met with a client, gave a meditation, or taught a class, my prayer was to be open to that right word—fully aware that on my own recognizance I was not capable of this level of work. This exercise gave me the peace and poise I didn't ordinarily have, and effectively placed me in the divine flow, from which, invariably, the right word came.

Gradually, as I built a clientele, I found it deeply satisfying to be providing such a service. Those clients seeking my help came with every problem imaginable—from acute and chronic physical ailments, to addictions, emotional distress, financial troubles, marital and/or family problems, as well as civil suits, property settlements, work-related issues, and business decisions.

My task was to clear my mind of a belief in the power of human conditions equal to God power. I must face down my own fears and beliefs in the power of any and all conditions and affirm my belief in a Power able to dissolve that condition. My treatments invariably included a request for divine right action and for perfect healing, whatever that might look like. Fully aware that, from my conscious knowing, I did not know what that perfect healing was, I appreciated a Wisdom that did know. It was to this deeper Wisdom within me and my client that I asked for healing and to which I acquiesced—not from my limited vision and human will, but from the greater vision and will of God.

In the client/practitioner relationship, I appreciated the church's rules and regulations that held the practitioner to a high level of integrity. Confidentiality was considered a sacred trust. We were expected to treat only those who asked for our help. We were *not* to treat those who did not ask. To take it upon ourselves to judge who might need or want our unsolicited help was considered gross misjudgment, manipulation, and control. Our intention was always to honor the integrity and sovereignty of the individual soul. Declaring the perfection of God in a person or situation, and stating that "there is only One Power, that Power is God, and that Power is Everywhere Present" was often all that was needed to separate myself and my client from the belief in the power of a present difficulty.

During those first years as a practitioner, I had many occasions to prove this new truth. Over the years I learned to do this well for others, but not always so well for myself. As a mother, I had always thought it part of my duties to fret over the comings and goings of my family. It was a great relief to finally realize I could pray prayers of protection, guidance and divine right action in their lives whenever I became uneasy about them. This gave me a sense of peace and knowing that God was in charge of each one—and all was well. Not only did this free me of my fears for their individual welfare, but, blessedly, set them free from my fear-thoughts.

During my practitioner studies program in the late '70s our son, Scott, along with about 90 other West Point cadets, were thought to be involved in a cheating scandal. Declaring his innocence, we believed him. Nonetheless, that didn't quell my fears that he might not be able to prove his innocence. A great deal of spiritual work was necessary on my part to feel that divine right action was taking place and that all would end well. While I had to work hard to build my faith and belief in divine justice, *his* faith was undaunted. He sailed through a long summer of litigation, positive that he'd be completely exonerated, and he was.

Several years later, our prayers went with him on a special assignment to Lebanon. While there, he witnessed the bombing of the U.S. Embassy from his hotel balcony. Since he always ate lunch at the Embassy, had he not received a dinner invitation for the evening and opted for a snack in his room, he would have been there at that moment. Again—when he was sent to Saudi Arabia in 1991 during the Gulf War, the family's prayers went with him. Not only did our prayers help us cope, I believe they were his protection throughout all of these crises.

These and other trials forced me to practice and prove the principles I was learning. If I hoped to be a successful practitioner, I must be adept at separating myself from a belief in the power of whatever difficulty I, or my client, was dealing with. If I found myself emotionally caught in a difficult situation where a loved one was involved, I asked my fellow practitioners and our Ministry of Prayer to speak the truth for me.

In 1980, our family moved from Oklahoma to the Pacific Northwest where I joined the Seattle Science of Mind Center. This was an active, growing congregation, headed by several ministers and an involved group of practitioners. Here I participated in the Ministry of Prayer, built a private practice, and over the next twelve years taught Science of Mind classes and other related subjects at the church. I met clients either in my home or at the church, also counseling them by phone and through correspondence. Listed in the *Science of Mind* magazine, I received calls from Florida, Texas, Oregon, Washington State, Washington, D.C., and Canada, as well as letters seeking counsel and prayer from inmates from several state penitentiaries.

But I was not prepared for the call I received one evening as I was preparing dinner. The moment I picked up the phone, this person began screaming, crying, and cursing God. My first thought was, "I don't know if I am qualified to help this woman. What can I say to ease her pain?" Actually, I couldn't make myself heard. As I listened to her raging, I suddenly felt such compassion for her, and a deep sense of humility in seeking for the right word to say to her. Thus, I was inspired to pray.

She had been so loudly hysterical, yet the moment I began to pray, a remarkable change occurred—she became instantly quiet. When I finished, she thanked me in a soft, kind voice and before she hung up acknowledged she felt at peace. What a profound demonstration of the power of prayer for this woman. Reminded again that the real work with clients is in the prayer itself, I gave a grateful, appreciative sigh. Normally, after a spiritual mind treatment, clients often expressed a sense of peace and release. Then later, further evidence of healing would emerge either as a change in the physical body, a mental or emotional shift, or guidance and new direction.

This, however, was not the case for another client who called frequently. A mother who believed it was her duty to rescue her husband and grown children from their addictions and problems with the law, she was often overwhelmed with worry and exhaustion. The matriarch of a large extended family, she couldn't get past her fears to actually place any of them in God's hands. I wanted to help her see a higher truth, but she couldn't quite grasp the idea of 'letting go and letting God.' Seeking solace and comfort, she simply wanted to share her sorrows and woes with me.

Dr. Holmes spoke of cases like this. He said, "Behind nearly every discord or disorder, there is some subjective complex or mental knot that needs to be untied." While the prayer/treatment I spoke for her brought a temporary state of peace, the peace was not lasting because she was unable to loosen and untie the 'knot.' Hers was a "no-win" situation that could only be resolved by a total surrender to Spirit. That was not going to happen until she could get past her fears and her belief that she was responsible for saving her family. Through our prayer work together, I led her to the truth, but I couldn't do for her what was hers to do for her true healing.

Indeed, this was how I managed to stay free from the issues that beset my clients. In the beginning, my husband was afraid I'd get caught in other people's troubles, which would undermine my own health and well-being. I had thought that might present a problem as well; however, it has worked the other way around. Affirming a higher truth for someone else, beyond their present experience, was often a healing for them and for me as well.

As I learned to affirm God in the midst of anything that appeared threatening, I noted that my fears would instantly dissolve and bring me into a wonderful sense of knowing when to act and when to be still. But, more than that, as soon as I declared Spirit as present in any difficult encounter, this silent prayer seemed to visibly alter the mood and demeanor of others who were involved, assuring a favorable outcome. Declaring Spirit as present in every person, as well as in every group situation, became a working hypothesis for me as a practitioner. I shared these ideas, and the story I had read of the Christian Science Student-Practitioner, with my students one evening.

At our next class session a student shared her experience of being at a coffeehouse with friends after our class the previous week. She left the table to make a phone call and was suddenly confronted by a big, tough-looking guy. Remembering the evening's lesson, she silently began affirming the God within him. In a matter of minutes, he shrugged, turned, and walked away.

Miraculously, she found that this simple shift in her perception, from outward appearances to an inner truth, had touched something inherently good within him, causing him to turn away. By silently seeing this man as a child of God, despite his behavior to the contrary, she defused an otherwise frightening situation. Not only did she bless him, she also found a right and safe way to protect herself. Quite a wonderful discovery!

Applying this principle to other situations, much to their delight and amazement, other students began demonstrating dramatic changes in their workplace and in their personal relationships. Every time they chose to see others from a higher spiritual truth they witnessed all manner of transformations. As a class we concluded that judging from outer appearances keeps us in bondage to our human problems, while judging from inner truth frees us.

When giving a spiritual mind treatment, practitioners place themselves under the divine harmony and will of God—appreciating that this will is for the highest and greatest good of all concerned. From this perspective, prayers are answered in a way that best serves the individual. Indeed, from our human perspective we cannot see what the soul needs. Although the perfect healing can sometimes be instantaneous; it can also be finding the inner resources to sustain and carry one through a present crisis.

While, from our human personality, we cannot control all that happens to us on this earthly plane, we can draw on our faith and belief in the invisible presence of Spirit and the unseen power of prayer to provide the spiritual resources we need to meet life's challenges. Understanding the power we have been given to consciously align ourselves with the love and light of Spirit; by speaking words of truth for the healing of our world, for our neighbors, our family and friends, we become a conduit through which God can work his perfect work.

Truth, as I now understood it, was that God's Love was infinite and available to all who asked, in faith, believing. Even though God's love is infinite, the law of God prescribes that we can have only what we ask for and what we believe we can have. Not understanding the giving nature of Spirit and the abundant good available to all, my clients typically limited their good by asking for far too little. Certainly the concept of God as Limitless Abundance seems beyond the grasp of most of us.

Somehow, we are made to feel that by accepting the good God has for us, we might be depriving others of their good. Many feel unworthy and even guilty for wanting a better, happier, healthier life. I felt that way once. However, the *Bible* tells us that "it is the Father's good pleasure to give us the kingdom." When we truly come to believe that, and know that *our* good is not someone else's good, we can help others believe it, too.

Without a doubt, this Love and Wisdom we call God has forever sought to express more of It's Love through us—that we might prosper and be in good health. It is wisdom to realize that God wants for us our highest and greatest good, yet we're not privy from our conscious knowing as to what that is, specifically. While we make our desires known to Spirit, we must make the added stipulation—"Not my will but Thy will be done."

When I came across these words of Goethe, a literary genius of the 19th century, I realized it described the work of any practitioner of truth:

> The chief thing is to have a soul that loves the truth and harbors it where it finds it. And another thing: the truth requires constant repetition, because error is being preached about us all the time, and not by isolated individuals, but by the masses. In newspapers and encyclopedias, in schools and universities, everywhere error rides high and basks in the consciousness of having the majority on its side.

* * *

As a practitioner, the emphasis in our training was not only in the art, science, and practice of spiritual mind treatment; we were also to "evoke true personal devotion and dedication," and a willingness to become a fit instrument for this vocation. As my professional life thrived, those years brought both joy and sorrow to our family. This was a time of the birth of our first grandchild, the marriage of our second daughter; the deaths of my sister, Judy, my father, and my mother-in-law. It was also the beginning of a trial period between my sister, Jeanne, and me.

Chapter 13

"...Thou shall love the Lord thy God
With all thy heart, and with all thy soul,
and with all thy mind.
This is the first, and great commandment."
Matthew 22:37,38

As a youth this commandment was a tall order for me since God appeared to be this remote figure, residing "up in heaven," far beyond the stretch of my imagination. *The King James Bible, 1611 Version*, was the one in our home, and perhaps that was why I couldn't feel a sense of connection to this God of my fathers, the God of the *Old Testament*. Although I found the stories interesting, they described events 3,000 to 4,000 years ago in a land half a world away. These narratives didn't easily relate to my world. Even in the *New Testament*, when Jesus made God more real through his teachings, this 'Father' God of the Old Testament remained an enigma. How was I supposed to love the fierce, judgmental God in these *Bible* stories?

Contemplating this commandment to love God—perhaps it meant to love that which is good, honest, and true. Emma Curtis Hopkins addressed this issue in her book, *Scientific Christian Mental Practice*, when she suggested we think of the word "good" whenever we think of God. Substituting the word "good" for God seemed to slice through the complexity of all the various ways people think of God, and gave me an image of God as encompassing all that I call good. In my studies, I had gained a larger perspective of the many attributes and powers associated with God: Creator of all life, Divine Mind, Unconditional Love, Universal Intelligence, Perfect Peace, Pure Joy, Wholeness, Oneness, Power—Omnipotent, Omniscient, Omnipresent. Meditating on these qualities fostered a deeper appreciation of this profound mystery we call God. I also liked Dr. Holmes's broader definition of God as Self-giving Spirit, giving life to all of creation.

Still, I realized that to love God with all that is in me required an awakening to the truth that God, in some wonderful, miraculous way, lives inside my heart. This awareness—that I am inextricably linked to this Loving Presence and the Divine spark within me is my connection to the creative power of God—is the greatest discovery of my life. Also, if this divine connection is true for me, it is true for all humanity.

Pondering my love for God, I used the following criteria. When I seek after truth and righteousness and all that is lovely, orderly, and harmonious, I believe I am loving God. Also, when I do to the best of my ability that which is mine to do each day—no matter how ordinary and menial—I feel I am loving God. As I listen to my heart and aspire to greater expression, as I search for peace of mind in the midst of chaos and confusion, as I ask for faith and trust in the midst of my fears and resistance, and as I look for the good in the worst of circumstances, I feel I am loving God. Years ago I read that we could know what we truly love by observing those things that fascinate us. Since my first encounter with the Light of Spirit, I have been unceasingly fascinated by the mystery of Spirit working in my life.

* * *

Continuing to explore diverse elements within Christianity, in 1985, I attended a five-day conference at the Brigham Young University campus on the Hawaiian island of Oahu. Billed as a Human Unity Conference in the brochure sent to our Seattle church, the presenters and the subjects to be covered sounded intriguing. I had been ecumenically oriented even in the 50's and 60's—and now here was a chance to meet people on the leading edge of Christian thinking. Finding myself in the company of citizens from thirty nations, representing many cultures and disciplines—all gathered here with a common vision—was a unique opportunity to learn and grow.

Among our presenters were religious leaders, scientists, scholars, authors, musicians, artists, and entrepreneurs to share their gifts and insights. Some represented the religious, scientific, and political perspective while others shared their expertise in holistic medicine, psychology, or the spiritual aspects of healing mind, body, soul, and spirit.

The major focus of the conference was to address the divisive nature that seems to separate our human family; within our different religions, as well as among our nations, cultures, and races. Our goal was to explore ways to promote a sense of peace and goodwill among all of God's children, in the area of spiritual unity, and to address global environmental issues as well. Troubled over the destruction of our forests and the pollution of our air and water, we wondered what could be done to ensure the quality of life for our human family and for all living beings? What could we accomplish in just five days to advance such a high purpose?

As these issues were discussed, I was amazed at how attendees seemed to appreciate and respect views quite different from their own. In an atmosphere of openness and trust, spiritual leaders and seekers alike discussed ways to live and work together for the greater good of all peoples and all nations. No one presented an agenda to convert others to their particular religious doctrine or philosophy, but all shared—openly and honestly their truth, and listened to others opinions and ideas as well.

Impressed by the talent, passion, and dedication exhibited as each person shared their creative ideas with us, I found their individual accomplishments inspiring. I found myself a bit envious of some of their achievements, and somewhat ashamed that I hadn't found a way to express my understanding of truth in a larger context, as they were doing. I couldn't comprehend this derelict feeling. Why did I feel there was something more I should be doing? I was very much involved in the Seattle Church, teaching classes, active in the Ministry of Prayer, and in private practice. Yet I couldn't shake the feeling.

The last day of the conference I joined an early morning meditation group to sit in silence within a circle of national flags on front campus. Leading the meditation was a petite, lovely East Indian lady dressed in a pristine white silk sari. Breathing in the salt air of the ocean and the beauty of this place, it took what seemed a long time to move my thoughts beyond the external to enter a quieter, deeper state of mind.

Just before the meditation ended, in my mind's eye, I saw a beautiful crystal skyscraper. Looking more closely, a woman was lying face down on the ground floor of this building. In the vision, she was unmoving, but alive. This was a powerful image, but it took a little time for me to decipher its message. I knew the figure was me—but why was I lying on the ground floor of this building—what did that suggest, and what did a "crystal skyscraper" represent?

As I contemplated this image some insights came forward. First of all, I sensed the crystal skyscraper as symbolic of 'truth,' and although I was 'in the truth,' I was not standing up in it. The question was—why was I not standing? Immediately I felt a strong fear—one that had been around a long time—the fear that if I stepped outside the church—to stand up in my truth in a more public arena—I would certainly face those who question and disagree with my understanding of truth. Was I ready for this?

While this image of 'lying down in my truth' was a revelation, it wasn't a complete surprise. It clearly revealed what I had been unable, and perhaps unwilling, to see before. Actually, the idea of writing about my spiritual journey had come to mind the previous year, but I had dismissed it. Some part of me felt the dreams and visions that were revealed, and the spiritual insights and blessings gained in the aftermath of my first encounter with Spirit, were meant to be shared. On my return home, I found a creative writing class.

My first efforts produced a brief perfunctory reporting of events as they had occurred. Class feedback was compassionately brutal, pointing out that in order for the reader to be drawn into my story I must share my innermost thoughts and feelings around these events. All agreed that the reader wants the drama, the intimate details, the "nitty-gritty," which at that point I was unprepared to give. I simply couldn't find words to express my deeper emotions. Having put a damper on my feelings for so many years, I wasn't sure I could get in touch with them again. The whole idea felt entirely too vulnerable and scary. Nonetheless, I began to write.

Swapping my typewriter for a computer, I started making little forays into the world of writing. I couldn't believe how many distractions and excuses got in the way. How did busy people find time to write books? My family, my practice, and my involvement with the Seattle Church left little time to start another project, and certainly not one this ambitious. Writing letters to clients, family, and friends was easy enough, but sharing intimate experiences with an unknown audience was quite another thing. The more I thought about writing a spiritual autobiography, the larger the project loomed.

Some part of me realized such an undertaking would be giving back in appreciation and gratitude to Spirit for the gifts I had received. The book would hopefully be an informative, enlightening, and perhaps even transforming experience for other seekers. Yet, another part of me was frozen with fear. Writing a book was so far beyond my idea of who I was and what I felt able to accomplish, I had to wonder why I had ever considered it in the first place. Perhaps the whole idea had not been of my conscious choosing, but rather a subjective one planted in my heart. Was it possible I was being nudged by Spirit, in spite of my fears and misgivings, to stand up in my truth? Certainly God knew my limitations.

* * *

Writers know that the process of writing is two-fold. First, one simply starts writing without judgment—without thinking about sentence structure, grammar, or transition statements—simply getting ideas down on paper—a right-brain exercise. Once this is done the inner critic is invited to edit what has been written—arranging the ideas into a proper flow of sentences and paragraphs that carry the story forward—a left-brain exercise. Not knowing this was the way it worked, I inadvertently allowed my inner critic to get the upper hand. A perfectionist, she showed no mercy, relentlessly hounding me with countless admonitions. Quite intimidating, her statements were on the order of—"Who do you think you are?" "You know, writing a book is big-time, way beyond your abilities; besides, you don't have the training, the talent, the discipline, or the credentials needed for success." Etc., etc., etc.

Every day I used affirmations, prayer, and meditation to lift my mind and spirits, yet in this instance, I became caught in all the reasons why I shouldn't attempt this project. I had the spiritual tools to quell the negative onslaught of fear before they established a beachhead, yet I failed to take immediate action. Now I couldn't get past their emotional charge. So immersed was I in these fear thoughts, I didn't even have the presence of mind to ask for help from my colleagues. Those negative voices were so strong, I quietly backed off. Instead, I kept up an appearance of writing, but stopped calling it a book.

When UCORS (the United Church of Religious Science) School of Ministry in Los Angeles decided to establish a branch at our Seattle Church in the late 80's, I put aside my writing, with a sign of relief, to become a student again. The subjects of World Religions, *The Old and New Testaments*, and particularly the teachings of Jesus, excited me. Courses in public speaking, psychology, the New Physics, and basic teaching and communication skills, also captured my interest.

When I completed these courses and it was time to learn about church management, administration, finance, etc., I realized the ministry wasn't what I wanted at all. While this side trip had been an opportunity to grow in greater spiritual knowledge and understanding, it had also given me a valid excuse to escape, at least for a time, the summons to write.

* * *

Clearly, fear has been the main issue in my life. Interestingly, those fears lay fallow until I began to walk the spiritual path in 1972. Then, when challenged to grow and change, they resurfaced. Every new belief was met by a fear-thought needing to be confronted and overcome. Was I ready to know the origin of these fears? Sitting in the silence with this question—seeking divine Wisdom—my thoughts went back to my childhood and my early memory of Jesus on the cross.

This image must have created in me a profound fear of God, as well as a deep fear of man's inhumanity to man. Why would God allow such a terrible thing to happen to one who loved Him so? These images were too mysterious for my child's mind to fathom. Had this terrible vision of Jesus on the cross somehow translated into another deeply held fear—that if I tried to follow his teachings, the same could happen to me? Did I have a fixation on those early images of Jesus on the cross? Was this why I was overreacting?

Then I recalled a bizarre dream that might be a clue to why fear held such power over me.

> The dream: Having entered a side door, I found myself standing in a center of a small Gothic-style gray-stone chapel. This building, narrow and high-vaulted, seemed to me an ancient family chapel long abandoned and empty, except for the five or six heads mounted on a side wall. Instead of stuffed, wild animal heads, these were heads of live, animated people. Although I didn't recognize any of them, I took them to be my ancestors. They were excited and all talking at once. Not able to hear what they were saying, I nevertheless understood they were issuing a warning of some kind.
>
> Leaving the chapel from this side entrance, everything was now shrouded in a gray mist, as though it was early nightfall. Walking round to the front entrance, I noticed it was completely overgrown with vines. The main entrance evidently had not been used in years, maybe not in centuries. Facing this abandoned and long-deserted chapel, to my immediate right was a small square pool of hot bubbling oil. Beyond this pool was a paved parking lot the size of a football field. Beyond that stood a long row of identical two-story houses seen from the rear—all shrouded in a murky gray. This large paved area was empty of cars, and not a single soul was in sight, except for a playful young monkey, dancing around this small pool of hot liquid. Obviously he was having the time of his life, daring to dance a little closer to the pool's edge each time around. I watched his antics until he finally came too close and fell in.

This dream, I believe, was portraying some great primal ancestral fear—a warning of what could happen if I stepped outside the bounds of church and family. (An interesting footnote: my maiden name is Bounds.) Suddenly my fears were seen in an altogether different light, showing me perhaps the root cause of at least some of my fears. Coming from deep, hidden places in my subconscious mind, I didn't know if they presented a real threat or were simply figments of an overactive imagination. Certainly, these fears had held me captive for years—standing in the way of expressing my true thoughts and feelings—and my new understanding of Spirit. Still, I was brought back again and again to the task of finishing this book.

It has taken a long time—and the patience of a loving God—to discover the extent of these fears and their power over me, and find ways to forge ahead. In the process, I've had to trust the leading of Spirit.

Chapter 14

"And the second (commandment) is like unto it,
Thou shalt love thy neighbor as thyself."
Matthew 22:39

To love God was one thing, but this second commandment—"to love thy neighbor as thyself" seemed much more difficult. Holding loving thoughts about people who had moral values much like mine wasn't hard to do; in fact, I found it relatively easy to think kindly of those who had similar likes and dislikes—who held a political ideology, lifestyle, or faith I could appreciate. But what about those who hold opposing views? Could I truly love those neighbors? I wasn't at all sure. Besides, how was I to identify "neighbor?" My dictionary gave two definitions. 1) "One who is located near or next to another" and 2) "a fellow human being." In this commandment I believe Jesus meant that, as fellow human beings, we are all neighbors, and therefore meant to love each other.

I felt we were loving our neighbor as ourselves whenever we performed simple acts of charity and compassion toward those in need; when we extended our hand in friendship to those next-door or halfway around the world; and when we truly appreciated our differences as part of the richness of life. Over the years, my husband's career took us across America, with a brief stint in England—giving us the opportunity to meet people from quite different backgrounds. Our experience could be called a testament to the friendliness of people everywhere. Although we naturally sought out neighborhoods that reflected our needs and values, nonetheless, our exposure to people from other cultures and religions, with different lifestyles, was very educational and broadening.

In the spring of 1987 I joined a group of about seventy people from Science of Mind churches in Washington State and California on a ten-day journey into Russia—specifically to Leningrad and Moscow. Here we met some distant neighbors, whose government we believed at the time to be a national threat to our country. Gorbachev was then head of the U.S.S.R., and although his regime was showing signs of easing the Cold War rhetoric, the Iron Curtain was still intact and President Reagan had declared the Soviet Union "the evil empire." Organized by Rama Vernon and Associates of Bellevue, Washington, our tour was like many she had made in the past three years. Rama's vision was that if ordinary American citizens could talk with ordinary Russian citizens beyond the scope of politics and the limitations of government, some of the distrust between our two nations might be overcome.

In the beginning, her motives and intentions were questioned by both the CIA and the KGB; however, by this time she had not only established an enormous amount of goodwill among the Soviet people, including the KGB, but she had also acquired a considerable network of Russian citizens eager to reciprocate. We were traveling not as tourists but as "citizen diplomats," ready to extend the hand of friendship to these "neighbors" from a Communist country. During a short stopover in Helsinki, en route to Leningrad (now renamed St. Petersburg) Rama and her staff shared with us what they'd experienced on previous visits, preparing us for the cultural shock we would encounter.

Our mission was to find common ground on which to build a working relationship with these people. For me the challenge was to get past the preconceived ideas and judgments I had garnered from the media and our government about Russia and her people. We were asked to try and hold two different points of view simultaneously—ours and theirs. That is, while holding our own position, we were to somehow put ourselves inside their shoes and see differences "with discrimination, but not with judgment?" It was a difficult exercise, to be sure.

Encouraged to keep an open mind and heart even when we felt we were getting "the party line," our questions needed to come from the heart and center on what we felt was important to them. If we found the conversation going nowhere, we could change the subject to children or hobbies and thereby set the stage for deeper discussions. These hints on how best to approach the Russian people and what to expect from our combined efforts boosted our hopes that something good could come of our mission.

Although we took advantage of the cultural and historical life of these two great cities, our main focus was visiting, communicating, and sharing with a cross-section of Russian citizens. Our citizen meetings, large and small, were held at the Friendship House in Leningrad and the Soviet Peace Committee Headquarters in Moscow. There we met a broad spectrum of society—teachers, parents, children, professors, doctors, businessmen, artists, musicians and performers. In these meetings we explored a wide range of issues. In addition, we met with a number of professional people who came to our hotel to speak to us. On a number of occasions we were invited into private homes for a social evening.

A highlight for me was an audience with the Bishop of the Danilov Monastery in Moscow, headquarters for Russian Orthodox Christians. (This compound is their equivalent of the Vatican in Rome.) Our group included two Religious Science Ministers and five practitioners. We were welcomed and ushered into an elegant yet austere conference room, as befitted such a historic compound, eager to meet His Holiness. When he entered, he was accompanied by several monks and a layman with notepad in hand. We immediately assumed this person was a member of the Communist Party there to monitor and take notes.

I was impressed by the Bishop's presence, sensing an aura of 'light' about him. Though stately and dignified, he was warm and friendly in his manner toward us, asking questions and listening to our concerns regarding a growing divisiveness among, as well as within, Christian communities in the United States and abroad. This issue was of concern to him as well. He seemed appreciative of our political and religious views as we were of his. At the close of our interview we were given parting gifts and a tour of the grounds. We saw their most ancient cathedral and walked through several newer ones. Each was magnificent and filled with ancient religious icons and incredibly beautiful art treasures.

The following Sunday was Palm Sunday and our itinerary included attendance at a Baptist Church service. Balcony seats were reserved for our group. From there we had a clear view of the choir on our right, the people across from us, as well as the sanctuary and altar below. Although the majority of congregants were older women, dressed in their heavy coats and babushkas (head scarves), there were young men, women, and children in the choir and audience as well.

Unable to understand the Russian language and what was being said during the two-hour sermon, we were nevertheless able to follow the familiar story of Palm Sunday from the tone of the preacher and the emotional response of the congregation. The hymns sung 'a cappella' by the choir, though unfamiliar, were exalting. The service ended with communion, where a large silver goblet was passed among us. Afterward, we were greeted outside by members thanking us for the gifts we had brought—a computer, Russian books and Bibles, art supplies, and miscellaneous supplies.

As was the custom in Russia, there was the usual exchange of souvenir pins. I had been saving my little angel pin for someone special. Suddenly there she was standing beside me in the crowd, dressed in her babushka, tiny and wizened with age. There was a definite twinkle in her eye as I pinned the little angel on her lapel. Giving me a bear hug and a kiss on the cheek, I momentarily turned away to regain my composure. When I looked back, she had disappeared. Afraid to show my feelings, I had hidden my tears. Had I not turned away this very special person would have seen how she had touched my heart.

On our last day in Moscow, our Intourist guide took us on a shopping tour. By this time, we'd established a friendly relationship with her. In a more relaxed mood, she confessed that the Soviet people were very afraid of our government as a threat to their peace. They looked on our great wealth as our power, and felt that their poverty put them in a weak and vulnerable position. When we told her the American people were just as fearful of them as a threat to world peace, she was absolutely stunned.

During this period, besides Rama and her groups, there were quite a number of church and business groups from the States on similar missions. The impact of these combined efforts are hard to evaluate, yet at the time they offered great hope and promise for the future of our two countries—and the world. Rama had quite literally—and on a grand scale—put into motion the commandment to "love thy neighbor as thyself." This journey into Russian territory and our interactions with the Russian people gave us the unique opportunity to experience first hand what it means to be a good neighbor. In a most profound way, it brought home the truth that peace and love begin with me.

I came home with a better understanding and appreciation of my Russian neighbors—people who were not yet free, but wanted to be. I also came home with a deep sense of gratitude for Rama's vision, and for her courage and faith in implementing such a mission. Being able to reach out to people who seemed so removed from our democratic way of life and to offer friendship took more than a vision. This endeavor took tremendous effort, dedication, persistence, and will.

I'm sure Jesus knew his simple statement, "to love our neighbor as ourselves," was anything but easy to follow. He understood the complexity of the human psyche, not only in sorting out our emotional reactions and judgments of others, but sorting out our feelings and judgments of ourselves as well. In this commandment he indicates that, although our tendency is to prejudge both our neighbors and ourselves, within our hearts greater resources for true forgiveness and unconditional love.

Although I've come a great distance on this journey of loving God, my neighbor, and myself, I have far to go. Clearly, my soul's work has been, not just about loving God, but also about loving my neighbor, and myself. My trip to Russia was a significant step in that direction.

* * *

Jesus, speaking in parables, said that "If a kingdom be divided against itself, that kingdom cannot stand. And if a house be divided against itself, that house cannot stand." {Mark 3:24,25) This universal law is a familiar axiom to many of us, yet we do not appear to understand its deeper implications. Today this great divide is playing itself out on many levels—within our personal relationships, in our religious and political institutions, as well as on the world stage in continuing wars and genocide. There will be no solutions to these large and small issues of life as long as we refuse to dialogue with our neighbors here and abroad. By listening, hearing, and respecting differing views, we will not only broaden our understanding of the world but find common ground among our neighbors to resolve our differences.

Somewhere along the way, our primal fears and moral biases for those who do not look like us, speak our language, and/or have a different ideology have kept us from following this edict to love our neighbor as God loves us all—*Unconditionally!* Even though this Commandment is a vital part of the Christian message (as I believe it is in other great religions) those of us who have held these Truths to be sacred but somehow unattainable may have been blinded to the highest truth taught and demonstrated by Jesus—***The Truth that Love is the key to the kingdom of Heaven.***

Chapter 15

"But I say to you, Love your enemies,
bless them that curse you, do good to them
that hate you, and pray for them which despitefully
use you and persecute you."
Matthew 5:44

Here was the ultimate challenge. Jesus had given us another commandment—to also love our enemies. What would have happened, I wondered, if our Russian neighbors had turned out to be our enemy after all; not an imaginary one, as we determined after meeting them? "Love thy neighbor" would then have become "love your enemies." Could we have loved them anyway? I wasn't sure.

When I left the Methodist church in 1973 and began studying the Science of Mind teachings, even after my sister informed me that I was involved in a "cult," I had not thought of her as an enemy. Actually, I didn't believe she thought of herself as my enemy either; yet there was no mistaking she was an enemy of this new philosophy. She simply couldn't believe Ernest Holmes was talking about the same God, the same Christ Jesus, and the same Holy Spirit as the one in which she believed. From my perspective, she and I were coming from opposite ends of the spectrum in Christian thinking, and there was nothing in her belief system that could accept another point of view.

I became aware of a growing number of people who were convinced that all "New Age" philosophies were cults, and as such, their followers were not "saved." I had already been challenged on this issue by total strangers in the Dallas airport in September 1976, returning home from my father's funeral. I remember this incident well. While waiting for my connecting flight, feeling pensive and sad, I became lost in thought as I watched dust particles suspended in a shaft of sunlight coming through a window high overhead. Caught in my own grief, I felt immune to the crowds and the senseless babble of voices around me. "Ma'am?" A male voice edged into my consciousness and I looked up to see two young men smiling down at me. Neatly dressed in black slacks and immaculate white shirts accented with straight, dark ties, they each held a clipboard. I struggled to focus, not wanting to be awakened from my reverie.

"We're taking a survey, ma'am. Could we have a few minutes of your time?" The voices were even and professional. Responding to their smiles, I smiled in spite of myself. "Yes?" I said. "Could you tell us, please, what church you belong to?" I should have been alerted by such a personal question from complete strangers, yet I had been caught off-guard and these young men seemed so kind and polite. My expression was open and friendly as I replied, "I belong to the Church of Religious Science in Seattle, Washington." For a fleeting moment I thought this might be an opportunity to share my joy at having found this teaching following my epiphany experience.

Immediately I felt a sense of foreboding as their smiles hardened into lines of disapproval. The amicable light in their eyes quickly grew cold, and then angry. "In the name of Jesus," one hissed at me, lowering his head to stare directly into my eyes, "How can you believe such satanic ideas! Don't you know this teaching is not Biblical? It is a "cult" and the work of the devil. May God have mercy on your soul." The other man added his bit by saying, "Pray with us now and repent of these false beliefs the devil has put in your mind and heart, and open yourself to God's forgiveness." Both men, by this time, were red-faced and shaking. They continued their harangue by telling me I should be grateful they had arrived in time to save me. By their cruel manner, there was no mistaking their aim had been to frighten me into conversion, then and there.

These young men called themselves Christians, but I saw no evidence of Christian love and compassion in either of them—indeed, quite the opposite. My stomach churned and my face burned from being slapped with their barrage of accusations. "Go away," I said. “Leave me alone.” Deeply offended by their self-righteous “we are right and you are wrong” attitude, I was also upset by this flagrant violation of my privacy. The entire episode was, as one might imagine, extremely unnerving. With trembling knees I stood to my full five feet, two and a half inch height, gathered my belongings and walked away, leaving them still preaching hell, fire, and damnation. They left the terminal that day minus at least one convert to their fear-based doctrine.

Safely on the plane, I gave in to the turmoil in which I'd been plunged. My hands were shaking as I fastened my seat belt. Tears came as I searched for a tissue. I felt an inner part of my being had been violated—as though thieves had broken in and stolen the last shreds of my calm composure. On my return home, it took a week to get past the negative charge I'd received from these brash young men. Needing to recapture an inner sense of God's presence, I spent much time in prayer and quiet meditation. Still grieving my father's death, these prayerful exercises gradually brought me into a state of inner peace. Out of these exercises I realized that “the peace that passeth all understanding” was inexplicably linked to my sense of God as an inner holy Presence. They seemed to be one and the same.

I learned yet again, from this difficult and painful ordeal, that when I get caught up in my own or another person's fear and negativity—I am immediately disconnected from my own sense of inner peace. In this confrontation I learned firsthand the truth that the mind is incapable of experiencing peace and fear at the same time. How quickly these young men were able to disturb my inner peace with their fears.

In June, following my spring trip to Russia, our family met on the Mississippi Gulf Coast for a reunion of first cousins. This day was a rare opportunity to reminisce and catch up with one another's lives, for remembering and appreciating our extended family. Mother, the last of her generation, presided over the festivities. The day passed quickly as we looked through old family albums, at the newest photographs of children and grandchildren, retold stories of other reunions—enjoying each other's company and the delicious food everyone had brought. Wanting to share the highlights of my trip to Russia, I had brought my album. No one seemed reluctant to look at my photographs or hear about my trip except my sister, who promptly stood up and, without a word, walked out of the room.

From earlier comments, I already knew she felt I'd deserted the Christian faith. Now, fourteen years later, not having returned to my religious roots, she must have felt everything I was involved in (including this trip to Russia) was highly suspect. During the intervening years she had discovered others who shared her same beliefs about Religious Science as neither Christian nor Biblical. Knowing that I was actively engaged in the study of Science of Mind and in the practice of meditation—both of which were not substantiated in the *Holy Bible*—she was deeply troubled. By now she was convinced I was a lost soul and, as my sister, she had an obligation to bring me back to Jesus. Later that same month when we were both visiting mother, she finally witnessed in person her faith and belief in Jesus Christ—restating the message of salvation I'd heard all my life.

The message was simple—all I needed to do "to be saved" was to publicly acknowledge Jesus as my personal Lord and Savior. The only other requirement was that I spell it out in the exact language of her particular religious dogma. My understanding was that, in her mind, nothing else would qualify. Actually, I found nothing wrong with the basic message she wanted to share. I too believed Jesus was the Son of God who had come to show us the way, the truth, and the light. What I found offensive was her insistence that she had the proper understanding of God's truth and I did not.

What's more, her approach was neither loving nor kind. Much like the two strangers who had accosted me in the Dallas airport, I sensed in her—fear and trembling. When I attempted to defend my beliefs, she became emotionally distraught and reduced to tears. At this point she began making accusations that were not only unfair and untrue, but were shocking and hurtful. In the next room mother heard every word. She'd always been proud that, as adults, her daughters seemed to get along so well. She was caught off-guard, as I was, at this sudden turn of events.

Since my spiritual encounter in 1972 in which I had felt the power, the presence, and the love of the Holy Spirit, my focus has been inner-directed. Traditional Christians are outer-oriented to bring others to Christ, and do not seem to understand an inner-oriented philosophy. They base their faith and belief in Jesus as their personal Lord and Savior, who died for the sins of the world—believing this is the *only* truth that can save humanity.

To my mind it is simplistic and totally unrealistic to think that all those who never knew, and will never know, the historical Jesus, or who cannot comprehend the idea of a God who could send his beloved son to die for their sins, are doomed to hell. To bring *every* soul to Jesus, even in today's modern world of computers and television sets, is not only a formidable task, but a seemingly impossible one. In my view, I believe we witness Jesus' message of unconditional love—not by proselytizing our particular religious dogma—but by loving God, our neighbors, and ourselves in ways that respect the sovereignty of every living soul.

I personally believe the nature of God has not withheld love, truth, or wisdom from his children in other religions and cultures. God has spoken truth to humanity through the *Judeo-Christian Bible,* and through the life and teachings of Christ Jesus, but I believe he has also spoken truth through the sacred scriptures and prophets in other lands, in other centuries—and to ordinary people today. For Christians, Jesus is the epitome of God's love, and held in high esteem by mystics of other religions as well.

Jesus found the kingdom of heaven within himself and sought to teach us this truth about ourselves—to show us how to live with one another—showing love, compassion, patience, true discernment, and forgiveness in all of our relationships. I believe the truth that will ultimately save us is seeking and finding this temple of the Holy Spirit within our hearts—there to nurture and cultivate these divine attributes.

* * *

I had never considered that one might actually suffer from the effects of harsh proselytizing, or from the misuse of prayer, until my encounter, first with the strangers in the airport, and then with my sister. I was shocked by a sudden realization that the power of the spoken word could have debilitating psychological and physical effects when directed by religious zealots toward sensitive, unsuspecting persons.

Until I had actually witnessed the dedication and determination of these groups to bring others under their influence—having experienced for myself their negative energy, their fears and resentment—

I would never have thought to call these people my enemies. Failing in her efforts to bring me to her way of thinking, I assumed my sister would finally be satisfied that she had done all she could do. But it was not to end there.

On her return home she launched an all-out campaign to "save" me—writing long letters and forwarding a profusion of tracts and pamphlets on "salvation." She also sent reams of material on the Antichrist nature of New Age Religions that included Religious Science. All the information she had gathered was, of course, from those who believed as she did. Predictably, their investigations confirmed that the Science of Mind was a "cult." (As I recalled from the *Bible*, didn't the temple priests consider Jesus and his followers to be a "cult?")

In one letter, she wrote of having taken a thirteen-week *Bible* course on cults at her church, followed by another twelve-week course on cults led by a non-denominational Christian ministry called "The Watchman Fellowship." In this six-month period, she believed she understood, better than I, what I'd been studying, working with, and experiencing as a positive healing for the last fourteen years. She was sure her sources were better-qualified and more credible to judge the truth or falsity of this philosophy than I. At this point, I was getting more than a little weary of this continuing saga.

In a very real sense, I was beginning to feel "persecuted." I had answered each of her lengthy letters with a lengthy letter repeating what I'd said before. Her response to my response was to repeat what she had already said. Sadly, in our numerous exchanges, no real dialogue ever took place. She was convinced that her interpretation of truth was not only the right way but the only way to salvation—and I was equally convinced of the authenticity and validity of my personal spiritual experience, as well as the feeling that Spirit had guided me into these new studies. We had definitely reached an impasse. Obviously we were getting nowhere, and so I chose to cease further efforts at reconciliation.

This cartoon, printed sometime in the 1980's, depicts precisely our delemma. Permission granted by the cartoonist, Mr. Eugene Mihaesco.

I began experiencing some very strange symptoms during the time my sister was engaged in this study of "cults," unlike anything I'd ever known before. The symptoms always appeared in the late afternoon and early evening hours, when I would feel a sudden draining of energy from my arms and legs. At these times, I could barely lift my arms or walk without assistance. But by the next morning, I would be much improved. In early August, we journeyed from our home in Seattle to Lake Tahoe for a reunion with our children and grandchildren. When the children saw me and heard a description of my symptoms, they were very concerned. Although physically and emotionally weak, I managed fairly well, and we had a wonderful week together.

However, on the last night of our vacation, this draining of energy came over me in a most frightening way. After dinner, I suddenly couldn't lift my arms at all and could not stand or walk unaided. Witnessing what I had been describing to them, my family was shocked at the weirdness of these symptoms. Unable to undress myself for bed, I was moved to tears. Terrified and wondering what could possibly be happening to me, I finally fell asleep. Following the usual pattern, I was better the next morning. Though still weak, I was at least able to dress myself and move about on my own. The previous night seemed like a bad dream, yet I knew it wasn't. What it was, I could not imagine.

Chapter 16

"Why beholdest thou the mote that is in thy brother's eye,
but considereth not the beam that is in thine own eye?
Matt. 7:3

The date was August 17, 1987 and the journey home from our Tahoe vacation took us past Mount Shasta. I remembered something I'd heard while in Russia about an event of cosmic proportions, called "the Harmonic Convergence" predicted to occur August 16th and 17th. This phenomenon was being hailed as a major planetary shift of some kind by those individuals who were psycho-spiritually attuned. Mt. Shasta, California was one of many locations around the world considered to be a sacred power center. Since this event was predicted to have great significance for the earth and for humanity, people had gathered here to pray and open to these higher energies.

Not being psychically attuned, I had no idea what this was all about; yet I understood that if these energies were coming from a universal source, which I called God, I wanted to be a part of it. Too weak physically to add even a bit of positive prayer as we drove past the mountain, I simply opened to the influx of these sacred healing energies. Stopping in Roseburg, Oregon for the night, we ate dinner at a restaurant across the street from our motel. On a bookrack by the cashier's counter was a book titled *The Seduction of Christianity.* I bought it perhaps to learn why the authors felt Christianity was being seduced. I could only read the first few chapters before turning out the light.

Hours later I had the following dream:

I was a janitor/caretaker in an old building that was our Religious Science Church. I was upstairs doing some office work when I heard a noise downstairs and went to investigate. I found this sad-looking woman sitting on the floor just inside the door. She had a small light beside her. I was reminded of the painting by Andrew Wyeth titled "Christina's World." This woman indicated that she'd come to bring us the light and, although I told her we had found the light within, I invited her to stay and speak to us. I began gathering chairs for this purpose. At this point the dream shifted. (This part of the dream was bathed in sepia tones.)

In the next scene I was standing in a large, empty sanctuary watering, with a long wand, a luxuriant profusion of vibrant colored fruits, vegetables, and flowers hanging from a bright, multi-colored canvas suspended from the ceiling.

The scene again shifted, this time to black and white. I was now outside the church building, walking toward a handsome, dark-haired young man who stood facing the church some twenty-five or thirty feet away. He was wearing black trousers and a white dress shirt. I stopped at his side to say these words, "We are both right and we are both wrong." Without another word, and not waiting for his comment, I walked away.

Then I saw myself walking out of this area into an open field directly south of the church building. To my right, at a distance, I noticed the skyline of a small city silhouetted against a glorious sunset. Looking overhead, I saw huge clouds in creamy rose and peachy hues billowing up and over each other in a most spectacular display. Transfixed by the beauty of these clouds, I watched in fascination as an enormous gold frame took shape around them. Then, I saw the head and shoulders of an "immense heavenly being" take form.

> As I watched, in total awe and wonder, a huge alabaster chalice was lifted by a 'heavenly hand,' and without warning, shot out of the sky in my direction. This abrupt action, so unexpected, jolted me fully awake—but not before I felt something as light as a clear bubble touch my lips.

* * *

Was this subtle bubble-like touch that of the chalice, now having shrunk on its earthward journey? In my mind's eye the chalice was suddenly reduced to the size of a small alabaster cup, similar to one I had bought in Russia just months ago. Beyond the obvious, I was only partially aware of what might be symbolized in these scenes. For instance, the first and third sequences seem a forthright message that neither my sister nor I had a complete understanding of truth—which, of course, was undeniable. The second sequence, where I am watering luxuriant and colorful plants suspended above our church sanctuary, was a riddle I would ponder later. Humbled and awed by such a powerful dream; even so, the first scenes paled in comparison to the spectacle of a heavenly being thrusting a giant chalice in my direction!

Could those dramatic and glorious images have come from the accelerated cosmic activity supposedly taking place at that moment, as well as from my mental, physical, emotional, psychic, and spiritual state of receptivity? "Wrung out" recently by the negative energies that had beset me, I was definitely open and ready to be healed. Was the image of the chalice a gift offering—and if so, what might that be? From sacred scripture and legend I recognized the chalice as a symbol of the Holy Grail. I felt the important messages, hidden within each sequence of this bold and extraordinary dream, would be revealed in time. In the present moment, however, I could only appreciate having been touched and blessed by such a profound and marvelous experience.

* * *

Home at last—needing to regain my equilibrium and strength—I put aside *The Seduction of Christianity*, to read at a later date. I concentrated instead on a physical, mental, and spiritual regimen of complete rest, meditation, and prayer. One day, several weeks later while running errands, I became aware of a gut-level feeling, a kind of inner knowing, that a shift had occurred and there had been some kind of breakthrough. I suddenly felt that strange malady I had experienced was gone. Although I couldn't explain how I knew, I sensed that, whatever those experiences had been, I was now free of them and their effects.

Because this draining of energy in my arms and legs was beyond anything normal or familiar, so unlike anything I had ever heard happening to anyone, I was left with some puzzling questions. Why had these weird symptoms appeared in the first place, where had they come from, why had they come only at certain hours of the evening, fading by morning—and lasting for a certain period of time before they were finally gone? Had I perhaps been a victim of autosuggestion? During this time period, the only clue I had that someone might have been seeking to influence me against my will was this struggle with my sister over my spiritual direction.

She was the only person I knew who had been diligently working for a long time to change my thinking and my beliefs. Nonetheless, as adamant as she was over the rightness of her beliefs, I didn't believe she would consciously wish me harm. In years past I had felt her negative energy directed toward me as a result of her personal belief that I was 'outside' the faith, but I had never felt any energy this strong—this powerful—and certainly not this debilitating. This level of energy seemed to be beyond the power of one person's prayer efforts; rather, a force generated by a large group of individuals.

Because of her determined and persistent efforts to bring me to Jesus, if these study sessions on cults had had a prayer list, it would have been perfectly natural for her to place my name on it. Nonetheless, I had no hard evidence that she had done so, and even if she had, I couldn't prove that my scary symptoms were a result of their prayers. Suddenly, I was struck with the realization that, indeed, prayer could be misused and misdirected by large groups of well-meaning and sincere people wanting to bring others to their understanding of salvation. Could unsolicited prayer actually undermine a person's health and well-being? This was a totally new way to consider the power of prayer, and it troubled me deeply.

A letter from my sister dated October 1987 says in part, "…you have not listened to anything I have to say about why Religious Science is completely contrary to God's plan." She goes on to say, "It was when you turned your back on Christianity that my hurt grew into resentment for it seemed as though you had grown to detest what we believed. At first I thought you had just rejected Christianity. Now I am not so sure that you rejected it, but just didn't know much about it." Further on in her letter she states, "I have spent a great deal of time in prayer and study in order to witness the truth of God to you. I do not regret one moment it has taken and would do it all over again, if need be."

When I first came into the Science of Mind Church I was surprised to hear a seasoned practitioner say she didn't want anyone praying for her without her consent. At the time I thought this a rather strange statement. Why would she not be grateful for the prayers of others? However, later in my studies, I began to see her reasoning. Like her, I wanted people to pray for me from a consciousness of God's Presence, God's Love and God's Will for me—not from their limited understanding, their pre-judgments, and their will for me. In my Science of Mind classes we were taught to pray for those who asked for our prayers. We were not to assume others needed or even wanted them.

* * *

Prayer is a powerful positive force for good when we are motivated from our highest concept of God, and when our intention is for the highest and greatest good of the person for whom we're praying. My personal knowledge of large and small groups coming together to pray for those who have <u>specifically requested</u> our prayers has been that great good has inevitably resulted. I first discovered the awesome power of group prayer in my Ministry of Prayer work with the Science of Mind Church in Tulsa. Years later, in a Brugh Joy Conference, I learned just how much power could be generated in any group attuned to a common purpose.

Now I was seeing another side of prayer—that behind our words might lie unconscious motives and intentions inconsistent with the fullness of God's truth. I would never have suspected that, even in the name of Jesus, prayer could be inadvertently distorted in an effort to bring others under the aegis of a particular belief system. For Christians who believe they must intercede on behalf of those they've deemed "not saved" is, in my opinion, a highly personal judgment that is not only intrusive, controlling, and manipulative, but also highly unethical. Those who believe they have the one and only interpretation of truth—that it is their Christian duty to bring those outside their faith back into the church (whether they want to be brought back or not)—should perhaps check their motives.

God grants each of us the sovereignty of our own soul, and I believe we are meant to honor that right in ourselves and in others. We have not been given dominion over the souls of others, but dominion only over our own soul. We are each, therefore, responsible and accountable for our individual life. To take responsibility for the spiritual lives of others, except in the case of parents of young children and caregivers of the mentally ill, is to take responsibility and accountability away from them—thus denying them the opportunity to grow in stature and in grace.

To think we know the heart, mind, and soul of another human being, or what God's will is for them, shows a gross misunderstanding of God's Love and Law. This tactic is essentially an attempt at playing God; for in truth, who can know the highest and greatest good for another? We can't even know this for ourselves. Only God knows—and when our prayers reflect this realization, we are praying aright. As a practitioner, in my spiritual mind treatments for clients, I was careful to close my treatments with this request—"for their highest and greatest good, whatever that might be." This approach felt in keeping with Divine love, Wisdom, and Truth.

* * *

Several months after returning home I finished reading the book I had bought in Roseberg, Oregon, titled *The Seduction of Christianity, Spiritual Discernment in the Last Days,* by Dave Hunt and T.A. McMahon. This was a startling revelation of the extent to which these writers believed in the widespread activity of the Antichrist. They said their intent was not to condemn but to rescue those seduced by Science, New Age religions, Holistic Medicine, and other "occult-teachings." From their perspective they see these teachings as a pathway to disaster. Adherents of the old school, they see the forces of evil hidden in what they call "pseudo-religions"—the sciences, psychology, and New Age philosophy.

The role of these writers is to warn of the prophesied "apostasy" and "sorcery" spoken of in the *Holy Bible,* which they see as evident in the sciences, and New Age teachings. (Apostasy is defined in the dictionary as an abandonment of one's religious faith, political party, cause, or principles.) They also believe healing through creative visualization is "sorcery." (Sorcery is defined in the dictionary as "the use of supernatural power over others through the assistance of evil spirits; witchcraft.") They fear that all human endeavors toward attaining a better understanding of our world and ourselves are about overthrowing God and becoming gods in our own right.

In defense of my experience of God as authentic and real and personal in my life, I take issue with their claims that God is not to be found in any of the above teachings. This book is a testament to the fact that on my path I found God's truth not only in the *Bible*, but also in places outside the confines of traditional religious beliefs. Using the powers within the human mind (a gift from our Creator, by the way), in league with the Mind of God, is not a clever ploy by the Antichrist to remake humans into "gods," but rather the activity of the Living Spirit—our inner Christ nature—preparing us to live our highest potential for the betterment of all life.

I also believe that evil is not inherent in the function and faculty of the imagination, but is, rather, in one's intention to misuse the imagination to deceive, control, manipulate, or harm others. Indeed, the gift of one's imagination can be used for *good or evil.* I, and the people I work with, consciously use visual imagery to see God's perfection in human conditions of lack, limitation, and suffering—in place of disease, in the midst of conflict, and in places where evil appears to dwell. We use the gifts of our mind and imagination as instruments of God's love and wisdom, seeking solutions to personal, communal, and world problems through prayer, meditation, and visualization—for healing the wounds of others and ourselves.

* * *

Jesus' commandments are these—Love God, love each other, and love ourselves—and yes, even love those we believe are our enemies. Here was another opportunity to find if I could really love those who kept pointing out the error of my ways, insisting they know better than I what is best for me. Even when people are unwilling to give me the freedom to follow the Light of Truth as that Light has been revealed to me—I am called to love them anyway. Even if they can't understand that I must do the thing that is mine to do, the thing that God puts on my heart to do—not what they are convinced I should do—I am to love them anyway. Even if I believe their misdirected prayers may have caused me undue suffering—I am to love and forgive them anyway.

With the two strangers in the airport, as with my sister, their approach to "saving" me was the very opposite of how Jesus would have approached me. If they had shown some degree of love and compassion, or even quiet reason, I believe I would have reacted differently. Instead, their strategy of coercion and intimidation was an insult to my intelligence. Their self-righteous attitude was proof enough for me that I was on my right path. Now, many years after the fact, I am still obliged to love and forgive those who continue to pray for my salvation. Why? Because I know they know not what is in my heart.

PART II:

BODY AND SOUL

Epigram:

"I said to the man who stood at the gate of the year,
Give me a light that I may tread safely into the unknown,
and he replied, "Go out into the darkness and put your
hand in the hand of God. That shall be to you better than
light and safer than a known way."

(From a plaque in St. George's Chapel — Windsor Castle)

Chapter 17

"For there is nothing hid, which shall not be manifested; neither was anything kept secret, but that it should come abroad."
Mark 4:22

Although in Biblical times much significance was given to dreams, no one in my world thought them important. In my youth and early adult life, I paid little attention to them, except to note their symbolic, ephemeral nature. For the most part, my dreams seemed benign, having little impact on my waking consciousness. All of that changed in 1972 after that astonishing spiritual encounter. After which my dreams sometimes appeared larger than life and fraught with meaning. Those I still remember with great clarity.

The dominant theme in my dream, described in Chapter 16, was a review of my spiritual journey so far; first, finding the Science of Mind Philosophy, and then a preview of something new being forecast. The alabaster chalice zooming out of the heavens seemed an offering and a gift from Spirit, yet there were no other signs to indicate what that gift might be. Had my startled reaction cut short this dream sequence? Would I have been given more instructions had I not been shocked into awakening?

Completely overwhelmed by the impact of this wonderful dream, I later came to realize that this dream was not just personal, but probably part of a larger collective dream as well—meaning that many people may have dreamed dreams and seen visions during the cosmic activity referred to as "The Harmonic Convergence." This bigger-than-life dream seemed highly prophetic—a rich field, full of further insights! However, with this dream still vivid in my mind and heart a year later, there was still nothing new on the horizon.

* * *

For at least a year prior to this dream I'd felt a vague sense that some of my spiritual needs were not being met; yet I paid little heed. Not knowing what lay ahead, I waited for clear direction. Aware that I couldn't make anything happen before its time, I returned to the work at hand. I became increasingly aware, on my trip to Russia, of the dramatic contrast between the weakness and numbness in my lower extremities and the positive energy operating in my upper body. Such a contrast clearly indicated an imbalance in my overall body system.

The lack of strength and energy in my lower body was no doubt due to the effects of rheumatoid arthritis (RA), while, most likely, the strength and energy in my upper body was the result of daily mental and spiritual practices. If this analysis was correct, I wondered why my spiritual practices had not healed my entire body. In its beginning stage, rheumatoid arthritis (RA) had been most prevalent in my hands, gradually spreading to my shoulders, elbows, hips, knees, ankles, and feet. My doctor, experimenting with different medications, finally found one that subdued my joint pain—keeping inflammation and stiffness to a minimum.

Except for the excruciating pain of that first acute attack in 1972, I marvel that I have suffered so little pain since that Epiphany experience. Despite some deformity, my hands and wrists are relatively strong—allowing me to write, perform most household chores, and otherwise live a normal, active life. In those early years, however, I did experience some physical pain, as well as a growing concern about the long-term crippling effects of RA. Learning to meditate was a great help in lifting my thoughts out of my pain and above my fears.

Still, I couldn't sustain this pain-free state of mind for very long. Once the meditation ended I'd soon be back where I started—in the same old pain pattern. Still, the practice of mentally abstracting up and out of my body into higher spiritual realms seemed a perfect solution to the problem of pain. As it turned out, I overlooked the real problem by managing—*to an unnatural and unhealthy degree*—to disassociate myself from my physical body.

The energy imbalance in my body meant that I'd favored certain aspects of my nature while ignoring other equally important aspects. Indeed, I had failed to appreciate a vital part—that of body and soul—as though they meant nothing. What I was now experiencing was a serious split in my psyche. In Religious Science, the primary focus is to know the truth of God as divine Mind/Spirit, to discover the power of prayer, and examine the teachings of Jesus as they apply to one's life. Although I had come to believe the truth of divine order, harmony, and balance throughout the universe, I had not taken those principles out of their mental and spiritual construct and integrated them into my own body and soul.

By concentrating *exclusively* on God and the divine spark within the human psyche, I had ignored the basic needs of both body and soul. Not only had I failed to appreciate my body and how it serves me, I had been negligent in the care of my soul as well. I knew nothing of who she was! In essence, the truth principles I learned in the Science of Mind was a necessary adjunct to my early Bible orientation. This expanded understanding of Biblical Truth helped build a solid foundation on which to grow. During those years of study, and seeking a personal relationship with the Mind/Spirit of God through prayer and meditation, my mind and spirit were healed many times over.

* * *

The "new kind of knowledge" that had been forecast in my dream a year earlier appeared in October, 1988, when Dr. Brugh Joy gave a weekend workshop in Seattle, Washington. I had heard good things about his work from friends in the Science of Mind Church—that his teaching focused on body energy work, and the "feminine mysteries," whatever they were. However, at the time this information didn't trigger my imagination or prompt me to inquire further. That was before "The Chalice Dream." That weekend I was introduced to a field of knowledge heretofore unknown to me—that of body and soul energetics.

While his workshop was designed to teach the basics of self-healing and self-nourishing, his greater intention was to bring us into a larger sense of "who and what we are." The large high school auditorium was packed that Friday evening. There were health professionals of every sort: nurses, nutritionists, psychotherapists, and healers of alternative therapies, as well as metaphysical students and teachers, spiritual seekers, and probably a few curious souls. Searching the crowd, I was surprised to find no one I knew. I was equally surprised to find so many people in the Northwest who were involved in the healing arts from a metaphysical, holistic point of view.

Dr. Joy set an informal tone by asking us to call him Brugh. He noted that he would explain just enough of the concepts he was introducing so we could begin to *experience* what he was describing. His exercises would provide a way for us to go in, individually and as a group, to touch something that really couldn't be articulated: a reminder that intellectually understanding a concept and actually experiencing that concept from a feeling level were *two very different things*.

That weekend he proposed that we might not be just a single person sitting in our seats but that our energy fields extended beyond our physical bodies. "Perhaps," he said, "we have resources beyond our wildest imagination, but don't know how to get to them. There may even be parts of ourselves that are actually heightened, healing parts that aren't in the ordinary awareness, and don't ordinarily operate through us."

Wow! At deeper, more subtle levels of being, I believed we were all one in Spirit and one with each other, but from a human perspective, I'd never thought of my body as an energy extending beyond my physical form. I thought of myself as operating exclusively within the parameters of my individual mind and body, and believed most people thought that way. Naturally, this information was startling. In our first exercise, he put us in touch with an aspect of our psyche that could *give* energy, then moved us to a different part that could *receive* that energy. Through this exercise, we realized the giving side of the psyche required a different mode of operation than the receiving side. This procedure required me to *feel,* rather than *think about,* what I was doing. Feeling something as subtle as this energy wasn't easy at best. With practice I hoped to eventually sense and feel it.

At the Saturday morning break, I found myself observing Dr. Joy from a safe distance. I was not, and have never been, a "groupie." I couldn't recall ever having met anyone I was overawed by, though there were many I admired and respected, so my reaction to Dr. Joy surprised me. Was I trying to determine if he was to be my next teacher? I had read his book, *Joy's Way,* some years earlier and found the material interesting but needing further explanation. Was he the one to guide me into "a new field of knowledge as suggested in my dream?"

* * *

For our Saturday session he had asked us to bring four photographs: a photograph of someone we loved, a picture of a total stranger, one of someone we felt had "done us in," and one of a sacred image. Right away, we noticed that each image triggered a different emotion. The question became: How could these photographs have so much power over us when we weren't even looking at the real person? From this exercise I learned a very interesting thing about the nature of the psyche. We were told that, "the psyche doesn't make a distinction between the presence of a real person and a photograph of that person. To the psyche, both are real and, as such, the images activate the same emotional responses."

Looking at these photographs—especially the one who had "done us in"—we were told that "our reactions were projections of *our own* shadow material—of conflicts going on beneath *our* conscious awareness." I had learned about projections earlier, but only as a mental concept. Fascinated by how each of the pictures evoked such different feelings, I had to wonder who was in charge of my psyche?"

For example, I was in one part of my psyche when I looked at the image of the person I felt had "done me in," and in another part when I looked at a photo of a loved one. Studying my sacred image—a picture of the ascended Christ—I felt an immediate shift in consciousness into a more heightened, transcendent, state of being—"one that offered redemption and forgiveness." As I looked from one photograph to another I was amazed to witness these shifts in my consciousness. From this exercise I gained an immediate respect for what some of the unconscious forces might be. Delving into how my unconscious mind works, and what might be hiding in those shadows, was to be a journey of self-discovery. I hoped I was prepared to take it. Understandably, I was having ambivalent feelings. I would be opening 'Pandora's box.' Yet, I might also be opening a new window of healing—*of seeing and of being.*

In Brugh's study of the energy fields of the body, called chakras in the Eastern traditions, he found the heart center uniquely different from the other energy fields. "This center seemed to be transcendent in nature, containing four sacred attributes: unconditional love, deep compassion, innate harmony, and the sense of a sacred Presence." He felt this heart-centering meditation provided the essential grounding for this level of body/soul energy work, and adopted it as the cornerstone for all his conference work.

He introduced us to this meditation by having us place our hands over our heart, calling forth the four attributes of the heart center and, at the same time, having us visualize this energy field as a radiance of light—flowing like an artesian well from an infinite Source. We were to *feel after,* rather than just think about, these sacred qualities. Then we were asked to see and feel this energy moving out of our heart center into our bodies as a radiant ball of light—out into our arms and hands. In a "*giving*" mode, we were to feel the light moving through us as warm and loving. Then, moving this energy through our hands back into our heart center, we were to feel our heart "*receiving*" this radiant light from our own hands. Moving deeper, we could allow the giving and receiving sides to fuse and meld, at which time we were to relax and just "be."

Brugh began each session with the heart meditation and used it again for the final healing ritual, when we attuned to a collective heightened energy—first for our own healing, then for the healing of others. We were informed that merging our energy with the energies of this larger collective would require a trust in order to overcome our feelings of vulnerability. Indeed, we would need to break the mindset of how we usually perceive ourselves and others, and, as he said, "begin to see that we are a most mysterious process."

As we began to break down the personal partitions that separated us, we became aware that, by turning our individual energies toward a group intention, as Brugh said, "the energy inducted would no longer be our individual energy, or his energy, but *all* of our energies merged. With the focused attunement of three hundred participants, the energy would be "squared," to an incredible *ninety thousand*!" With so many people engaged in the closing ritual, at first I wondered how this would unfold. However, once I felt the attunement, and the giving and receiving of this radiant, loving energy, I realized the healing power generated in such a large group ritual.

With a little maneuvering, Brugh led us into this final ritual, dividing us into circles of eight. Then, beginning with the heart-centering meditation, he took in and out of circles, while we gave energy to and received energy from each other. Our coordinated movements became a beautiful dance—a moving art form—that carried us into an awesome sense of oneness with each other.

At the close of the workshop, I felt I would work again with this teacher. *

* Appendix A (Brief Bio of Dr. Joy)

Chapter 18

"... Awake thou that sleepest, and arise from the dead, and Christ shall give thee light."
Ephesians 5:14

Two months after my first workshop with Dr. Joy I attended a five-day conference with daughters, Sally and Laura, at Asilomar, a beautiful retreat center in Pacific Grove, California, near Monterey. We joined more than three hundred people to celebrate the year 1988 ending and a beginning new year with Dr. Joy and David Spangler. Thrilled to be together for such an occasion, we looked forward in anticipation to the outstanding presenters and programs Brugh and David had assembled.

Asilomar was ideal for a spiritual retreat of this size. Secluded from local residences and businesses by acreage and fences, it offered both luxurious and modest accommodations. The buildings, including a spacious lodge and assembly hall, had rustic exteriors but were furnished with modern amenities, including a large, full-service dining hall. The complex, nestled among tall stately pines, gave the impression of a wilderness retreat—which indeed it was—even amid the bustle of city life just outside the gate. Incredibly, a natural quietness pervaded the air. In addition, the Pacific Ocean was just minutes away via a footbridge over the sand dunes. A perfect setting for mental and spiritual renewal.

Brugh and David had been holding these year-end conferences at Asilomar for a number of years. The theme this year centered on "The Mysteries"—of mystery schools and mystery training. Their aim was to provide a setting where founders of mystery schools from different spiritual disciplines could share their wisdom. Their greater intention was to create a sacred environment that would not just touch the life that flows in and through us individually, but touch the mystery of Life Itself.

Months of planning brought artists and technicians together to create a sacred space in the main hall—a space that would call those who entered into a sense of something deep and profound. Through the magic of light, color, and sound, an altar to the "Alchemist" took form. Brugh and assistants had choreographed every detail to awaken us into a sense of the sacred and bring us, as Brugh said, "into higher ranges of our being."

In addition to the latest technology in stereophonic sound, we were privileged to have two "in-house" artists sharing their talents—David Whyte, a marvelous poet and storyteller, and Susan Osborn, a gifted singer and composer. Introducing each speaker, they set the stage by heightening our awareness of the transcendent. Brugh and David, in their welcoming comments, confessed that, although their programming had a solid framework of presenters and performers, beyond that, how the week unfolded would be as much a "mystery" to them as it would be to us.

As the lights dimmed Brugh brought us into our heart center—"to touch and explore, to deepen and celebrate, to attune and appreciate how deep a mystery life truly is." A short period of silence followed. Then stereophonic sounds transported us—through magnificent sacred music and the voices of a Gregorian choir—into the great cathedrals and temples of the world, softly at first, and then resoundingly—carrying us into another dimension.

When the music faded, both David and Susan took us more deeply "into the mystery" with their compelling poetry and song. Susan then introduced our presenter for the evening—Rabbi Zalmon Schechter, also known as "Rebi," and his partner Edye. These two "Jewish mystics" founded a mystery school in Boulder, CO based on the Jewish mystical tradition of the Kabbalah. Brugh explained what mystery schools were all about, telling us that "mystery school training has nothing to do with secret formulas or secret statements but with awakening into our inheritance—what we have been gifted with by right of having gained existence."

Rabbi Schechter reiterated that point, saying, "Our school is designed to awaken those who are ready to enter the vast interior of

'Beinghood.' The focus of their training was not about Judaism but about "our oneness as a human family—and the need to encourage that oneness in our world." To facilitate that awakening and feel our connection with each other as a human family, Rebi and Edie led us—three hundred strong—singing and chanting sacred verse, moving and dancing "as the Spirit moved us." As the chanting and movement continued—building a heightened sense of joy and well-being within us—we began to feel our collective energies interweaving. At the close of our first evening we were left with deep feelings of appreciation and gratitude for life—and, indeed, for its mysteries.

The following morning, David described our next presenter, Dr. Jean Houston, as a poet of the mythically human. Dr. Houston shared interesting insights into her spiritual awakening and her background as a student of the great German theologian, Professor Paul Tillich. She founded a mystery school on the East Coast out of her Sacred Psychology studies. Her travels into different parts of the world and into many diverse cultures had given her deeper insights into this mystery we call Life. Her basic message pivoted on this theme: "Awake thou that sleepest—awake to the mystery of life."

With the assistance of a classical Shakespearean actress and friend, Margeret Nash Reuben, Dr. Houston enlivened her presentation powerfully by dramatizing the hidden wisdom that has come down to us through myths and legend. She also gave us new ideas to contemplate as she shared her intuitive sense that "the genius of the feminine spirit, which exists in both men and women, is transforming from old warrior archetypes to something new."

Time alone, and time to enjoy the company of others, was provided each day. The opportunity to walk along the beach—alone and with my daughters—to bask in the sights and sounds and smells of the ocean—dovetailed perfectly with the theme of the conference and this mystery of life. Walking barefoot in the soft warm sand that turned cold and hard-packed at the water's edge, we watched sandpipers dash along the edge of outgoing waves in search of food. Breathing the clean salt air, welcoming its spray on our faces, hearing the squawking of sea gulls in the distance, and gazing in fascination at the never-ending waves breaking on shore, left us in awe of this great body of water we call the Pacific Ocean.

* * *

Brugh and David were our featured speakers on a number of evenings. Sitting casually on the steps leading to the stage, they created an easy give-and-take of ideas between themselves and with us. These conversations were often humorous, and always enlightening. We appreciated their radiance, their insights, and their clarity. Not only did they have great respect and appreciation for Life's mysteries, it was obvious that both had been greatly blessed by its mysteries. David's background in college was in biology and biochemistry. Therefore, he often used metaphors and images of cells and other biological phenomena in his approach to the mysteries.

David's comments:

> He talked about our DNA as a "mystery school" at work in every cell of our bodies—receiving energy, giving energy, storing energy, harnessing energy." He believed modern science was "an outgrowth of the mystery tradition, citing many of the great minds that fathered the Scientific Revolution as mystics, metaphysicians, and theologians." He continued, "In the beginning, the scientific idea was to make accessible to the common person a knowledge that, whatever the country or culture, the answer would be the same.
>
> Through investigation and experiment they began to discover truth, which is essentially what the scientific method is all about. However, in a very real sense, particularly in western society, the world turned inside-out and the objective world became "the measure of truth." When he said "the world turned inside-out," David was indicating the fact that before the Scientific Revolution the sacred/mystical/invisible/subjective world of Spirit was considered to be the source of universal truth and wisdom. But after the Scientific Revolution there was a dramatic shift in Western thinking to believe in the physical/material/visible/objective world as the 'measure of truth.'
>
> David further indicated that the esoteric, or inner aspects of mystery training, represents a body of knowledge and

> insights that one has to pay a price to acquire. "If you are willing to pay the price, then the knowledge is yours. Medical doctors, nuclear scientists, brain surgeons represent the esoteric to many of us. In the esoteric 'mystery' schools, there are prices to be paid. It is not that the knowledge is hidden or forbidden, but the price to acquire the knowledge is more than most of us are willing to pay."

At this point, David turned the mike over to Brugh who began by saying that "the fundamental task in mystery training is to know thyself."

> He said, There is a long journey in the awakening and the apprenticeship into mystery training. It requires a long period of patience and the alchemy of learning timing—of learning the interrelationships of forces. There is a time when you must set aside all the great movements you know about in the world and let others take those for a while, while you learn the deeper mysteries of your own being lest you go out and create more problems than were there in the first place.
>
> We are not a single individual—indeed, we are many selves interiorly. For instance, there might be a rational part of you that hopes you will be part of those who go out to save the world. However, you may find that that particular "part of you" is way down on the totem pole of possibility—just a little dot in this vastness of beinghood and it has to take its proper place. This can be a big shock when we have to give up being 'numero uno.'
>
> Brugh emphasized the point that "fundamental to the mystery training is learning that we are not 'numero uno.' We find there is something else that is 'numero uno.' This is where Spirit comes in. We find there is something beyond anything we can cognate or conceive that is the essence and source of our being."

The third morning of our conference, Dr. Gay Luce, founder of The "Nine Gates Mystery School on the West Coast, led us in a guided meditation to a background of soft music and beautiful images projected on a large screen. The key, we were told, was to "look not at the images, but look for the meaning *behind* the images, to get a sense of what was at work in our psyche." For me, this was a new and somewhat difficult undertaking.

Following this meditation, Brugh spoke further about the power of an image to evoke certain memories and/or emotional responses that, in fact, can bring us into a greater sense of who and what we are interiorly. I recalled from his workshop looking at the different images Brugh had asked us to bring and how very different my responses were to each one. This exercise allowed me to see what I had never seen before—my emotional response, not to actual persons, but to photographs of those persons.

Dr. Luce was our main presenter the following morning. Talking about the power and importance of ritual as a way of remembering our spiritual heritage—she led us through a series of rituals where drumming, chanting, movement, and dancing, and invocations were called into play. Through the act of sacred ritual, humans can touch places that cannot be reached through ordinary states of consciousness—for healing and integration. Again she reminded us that "ceremonies and rituals act as vehicles of consciousness to take us into our inner temple."

A portion of one day was set aside for silence and fasting. We were to remove ourselves from verbally interacting with others long enough to assimilate the wonderful "trans-ordinary" experiences we were having. Eye contact, smiles, and nods were permitted and encouraged while we kept the silence. Sally, Laura, and I struck out on our own to explore what this period of silence could bring. Our experiences differed, of course, but were deeply significant to each of us.

* * *

Patricia Sun was a name I'd heard mentioned among my peers and, although I wasn't familiar with her work, I was delighted to see her listed as a presenter. A spiritual teacher in metaphysical circles, she shared her knowledge of the mysteries the fourth morning. At one point on her spiritual journey, she was told that her voice could be trained to tap into ranges far beyond what is considered normal for the human voice. The highlight of her presentation was a demonstration of this amazing gift. Awesome sounds coming from her throat seemed to originate from some faraway time and place. Incredibly, each note carried a resonance and tone that was not only powerful, but that she held for unbelievable lengths of time. Definitely, something deep and powerful was being shared with us.

* * *

As the conference drew to a close, I realized that every one of our presenters had spoken of the need to awaken. In such a perfect setting as this, many of us had been awakened on some level to the various mysteries. I was pleased that both Sally and Laura had such rich and meaningful experiences to take with them. Although my experiences weren't as dramatic as theirs, I did have many wonderful quiet moments to savor and reflect upon. I had gleaned much from each presenter—and from Brugh and David—to ponder in the coming months. As a result of this conference I looked forward to again working with Brugh.

I asked Sally and Laura if they wanted to share their thoughts and experiences from the conference as well. The following is Sally's experience:

> It was magical for me. I was ready for transformation. Open, trusting, and innocent—I felt safe that I could let go with Brugh and David leading us, with you and Laura by my side. I also felt a special kinship with this place. My peak experience was during Gay Luce's afternoon workshop. I remember walking in a circle a certain number of steps to set a sacred space. Gay made her way around the circle to each of us (about 50 or 60 people, maybe more) and sprinkled us with a fir sprig dipped in water. A young man followed behind her—beating a steady rhythm on his Native American drum.
>
> A significant moment for me came when Gay had us turn to the person standing nearest, place our palms together, look into one another's eyes, and send the other uncondi-

> tional love. I felt great love and compassion as I looked into the eyes of the slightly older woman who was my partner. Almost instantly I felt a powerful surge of energy. It blew from inside of me out, through the top of my head, through the bottoms of my feet, through my heart—through everywhere really. It was like a flash flood and a bolt of lightning. My partner burst into tears and I burst into light. "Afterward, as I wandered, stunned and recovering, Brugh came up and gave me a long hug. I guess he saw all that light.
>
> From Laura: I felt very connected to the people attending and very enlightened by the speakers/presenters. I remember laughing a lot at dinnertime. There was a wonderful feeling of joy and anticipation. I still remember Susan, our singer with the incredible voice, who sang and shared her story of singing in a chapel in Italy and how astonished she was at the way it sounded. But the most amazing event for me was the healing circle that sent me up and out—when I found myself transported into outer space, circling the planet earth with a host of angels. I thought everyone had had the same experience—that this was the whole point of the healing circle—only to find that everyone was having an experience different from mine.

The circle Laura described was the final ritual of the conference. Brugh had divided us into groups of eight. People in these groups came together under his direction to give healing energy to, and receive healing energy from, each other. The ritual's energy built as each person took their turn lying on a table in the center of the circle to receive healing energy from their group. She was the last in her group to receive this energy and by that time, it had built in intensity and power. As a result she was gifted with this most incredible sense of circling the earth with angels.

* * *

The following poem, written and read by David Whyte, summed up for me the power of the awakening Spirit.

The Opening of Eyes

That day I saw in the dark clouds
the passing light over the water,
And I heard the Voice of the World
speak out and I knew then, as I had before
Life is no passing memory of what has been
nor the remaining pages in a great book
waiting to be read.

It is the opening of eyes long closed.
It is the vision of far off things
seen for the silence they hold.
It is the heart after years
of secret conversing
speaking out loud in the clear air.

It is Moses in the desert
fallen to his knees before the lit bush;
It is the man throwing away his shoes
as if to enter heaven
and finding himself astonished,
open at last,
fallen in love with solid ground.

-from Songs For Coming Home
by David Whyte

Chapter 19

"Yea though I walk through the valley
of the shadow of death
I will fear no evil..."
Psalms 23:24

In the spring of 1989, following the Asilomar retreat over Christmas week, my mother died. I wish to share some thoughts and feelings around the issue of death—and the grieving process as I have experienced it, not only with my mother, but also with other family members and friends who have gone before. Try as I might to escape the physical reality of death as I was growing up I could not forever stay in denial of this truth. Life on this physical plane does come to an end sooner or later—and like everyone else I must accept this fact. Mother was right when she said, after the loss of my paternal grandmother, "Death is just a part of life," yet this information did little to enlighten or comfort me.

Blessedly, I have grown past my early fears of death with the realization that the life of Spirit is the reality behind and beyond what we call physical death. Even so, the painful process of grieving the loss of family and friends remains. Deeper understanding did not dissolve the pockets of sadness I felt with each loss. Now I see that our human experience of death is only a partial and very limited view of an event that ultimately leads into a new and expanded dimension—the dimension of Spirit. Whatever death is, I see it now as only a shadow—as the Twenty-third Psalm so beautifully describes it.

While I no longer fear the passing of life from this plane into the next, it was not always so. As a child I ran away from the idea of death, unable to sort through my fears and misgivings about what lay ahead for the deceased. The thought of dying and existing no longer was too deep a mystery. As a young adult I still had not developed an adequate measure of self-control nor appropriate words to offer the bereaved. In my own grief I was often left temporarily numb and speechless. Rather than being a comfort to the grieving family I needed someone to comfort me—to hold me and reassure me that life was ongoing and everlasting; to realize that death was simply a doorway into another dimension free from human cares. Although my parents believed life was ongoing, they were stoic, and silent, on the subject of death.

* * *

At eighty-four, mother was still living in her home in Hattiesburg, Mississippi and fiercely independent. She was known for her culinary skills—the caterer for many years for the three-thousand-plus membership of the First Baptist Church—and in the community at large—for wedding receptions, bar mitzvahs, corporate parties and banquets. She loved her work, excelled at it, and strongly identified who she was through her profession. Throughout her life she had enjoyed good health until, in her late seventies, after two knee surgeries and a hip replacement, she reluctantly accepted the fact that she could no longer fulfill the demands of her job.

Retirement was a major adjustment. Although family, friends, and neighbors called and dropped by often and she could still drive, she had no experience sitting on the sidelines watching the world go by. I doubt her active mind was fully satisfied with the daily routine of newspapers, crossword puzzles, and television. My sister and I lived in distant states—too far for frequent visits but her brother, Spencer, visited often, spending several days at a time doing little odd jobs for her.

* * *

I was with her during and after her first knee operation. She fared quite well during the first days of surgery, yet when time came for physical therapy, the pain was so intense she wanted no part of it. She was temporarily in a kind of "twilight zone," seeking escape from the pain, unable to realize that, without therapy, she would not walk again. I had recently taught a class using lessons from the book, *Scientific Christian Mental Practice,* by Emma Curtis Hopkins. She had written that there was a "right word" for every occasion. Yet that word was never revealed because it was different for every person and in every circumstance. The key was to be open to the right word for the moment.

I felt my mother needed a "right word" for this new challenge. I prayed, both for her and for myself, to be open to whatever that right word might be. Entering her room the next morning, without any forethought, I heard myself make the following statement in a strong, commanding way: "You have worked all your life taking care of everyone else in the family. Now that you're free to pursue the things you'd like to do, you aren't able to walk." I was not giving advice but simply stating a fact.

I could see that what I'd said, and the way I'd said it, had gotten her attention. Later that morning I detected a subtle shift in her thinking, from feeling desperate to perhaps a new sense of "I can and I will." After that, she was cooperative and appreciative of the therapist's help and was soon up and about on a walker. When I later reviewed what I'd actually said to her, my words in no way resembled a typical healing prayer or affirmation. However they were apparently the words she needed to hear—reminding her that she still had a life and she could live it more fully.

Jeanne and I brought up the subject of coming to live with one of us or, if she chose, alternating between the two of us, as her mother had done. She emphatically refused to consider such a thing. To her mind, this was simply out of the question. Hattiesburg was *her* town—where *her* friends, *her* church, and *her* doctors were. Besides, she protested, she could still manage on her own. Her later surgeries were met with resolve to stay as independent as she could. This she was able to accomplish. But by then she was already beginning to experience some physical unease.

Actually, I could understand her not wanting to give up her home and her freedom to be displaced to another state and another city. She'd have to fit into our lives, even if we were family. At that point she seemed years away from being a candidate for a nursing home, yet Jeanne and I both knew her great fear of nursing homes.

She had heard stories from friends and neighbors of mistreatment and abuse in several local nursing homes. Whether the stories were true, hearsay, or just plain gossip, they inflicted terror in her heart and mind, and in the hearts and minds of her friends and acquaintances.

With time on her hands, she may have worried too much over what the future might bring. She, no doubt, was also saddened over the "religious argument" between Jeanne and me, although she never brought up the subject, nor did I. I knew from my own experience that unrelieved stress over issues beyond one's control could have a devastating effect on one's physical and mental health. I prayed for her inner strength and faith in God to lift her above any and all disturbing thoughts and feelings to a place of peace.

Much of the last three months of her life was spent in and out of hospitals as doctors tried to determine the cause of her pain and discomfort. In our phone conversations she told me that neither she nor her doctors were greatly alarmed. They assumed that whether it was her gall bladder or "some other thing" they couldn't name, it would eventually show up in a test—at which time the right medication and/or operation would take care of the problem. When a barrage of tests still couldn't pinpoint the problem, I scheduled a trip to see her. She was out of the hospital by then, and self-medicating whenever she felt a "little heartburn." I was, of course, disturbed by this state of affairs, yet I never expected this would be our last time together.

While she seemed okay during the day, every night she'd have a bout with what she called "a bad case of indigestion." Still, we had two wonderful days together. Two of her favorite nieces (and my favorite cousins) came from out of town for an afternoon visit. I can't remember a time when my mother was so animated and full of life as she was that day. Listening to her as she recalled stories we'd forgotten, or had never heard before, we giggled and laughed so hard, we cried. She obviously overdid it. By bedtime, she was extremely uncomfortable. She doctored for heartburn and indigestion and when these didn't work, she took a digitalis tablet.

When I suggested we either call her doctor or go to Emergency she chose to wait. (So used to making her own decisions, I knew that, even if I had insisted, she wouldn't have listened.) Sure of my mother's intuitive wisdom—the wisdom that had served her so well all the years Judy was ill—I accepted her decision to wait. Sadly, we both failed to heed the warning signs. Listening for sounds of wakefulness during the night, all was quiet. She may have been hurting, but determined not to call for help until morning's light. When I checked on her at daybreak, she finally allowed me to call her doctor, who ordered an ambulance and said she would meet us at the hospital. Arriving at the hospital, her lungs were already beginning to fill with fluid. She died minutes later in the emergency room.

My first reaction to her death came as somewhat of a surprise. Not until I tried to call my husband and couldn't remember my own telephone number did I realize I was in shock. Although I managed to drive from the hospital safely back to my mother's home, inform family and neighbors, and carry on other duties, a part of me remained in a strange sort of stupor for several days—seemingly together on the outside but, on the inside, devastated. At the same time, on yet another level, I was sensing her spiritual presence as very real—which was a great comfort.

Mother died on Palm Sunday. Many people came to pay their respects, bringing food and sharing stories of their friendship with her and what she had meant to them. Two incidents attest to the kind of person she was: once when she fell and broke her arm, while lying on the floor waiting for the ambulance, she asked her sister-in-law, Lil, to bring her the phone, at which time she placed a large order for catering supplies. Even on the fateful morning of her death, as the medics wheeled her out the door on a gurney, she was giving me instructions on how to lock the house.

Her funeral service was held in the beautiful sanctuary of the church she had served so long and so well. The Easter lilies, displayed en masse above the altar in readiness for Easter Sunday, remain a vivid picture in my mind of my mother's faith and what she meant to her family, her friends, her church, her community—and to me. When I returned home to Seattle later that week, I was amazed that I could feel her presence. By contrast, when she was alive with so many miles between us, I was ever aware of our physical separation. Now I only had to think of her to feel her near. She has been gone now for many years, but when I think of her she still feels close.

* * *

Earlier encounters with death caught me unprepared. In the early Sixties, when an old friend called long-distance to tell me that a close high school friend of ours had died, I was not only stunned that breast cancer had claimed Katherine's life at age thirty-five, I was also distraught that she had left two young children without a mother. Overcome and bereft of words to comfort her husband, I failed in my obligation to call or even write to him. He would have appreciated knowing how much her friendship had meant to me in our teen years.

Soon thereafter, I lost another friend to cancer. Roberta and I were 'Kiwi' friends in Tulsa, both having been stewardesses for American Airlines. She, too, was in her thirties—the mother of two young children. Paying our respects, C.B. and I visited her husband, but neither of us could voice our admiration and appreciation for his beautiful wife, fearful of losing control of our emotions. So strong were my feelings, I wondered how her husband, Dale, was able to talk about her. Had the deaths of these close friends triggered deeper fears in my subconscious mind about the possibility of my own death at an early age—leaving behind my children? I didn't know.

Then in the Seventies, my close friends, Bobbie and Ingram Foster of Prentiss, Mississippi, lost their oldest son, a college student at the time, to cancer. I knew of his illness months before his death, but again, imagining their pain and not knowing what to say to console them, again I failed to call or write. Not only was I remiss in expressing condolences to Bobbie and Ingram, I was also struggling with my inability to give comfort to Judy and to my parents at the same time. Again, my inability to express my love and sympathy to my friends, and to my own family, was inexcusable.

* * *

On a number of occasions when Judy was near death none of us could bring ourselves to talk about the possibility of losing her. We were all in denial of the fact I believe, except mother. From the manner in which she held herself and the family together she may have known intuitively the truth and girded herself, psychologically and spiritually, as best she could for the inevitable. Yet she couldn't broach the subject. We were each left to draw spiritual strength from within our personal faith and belief in God.

Despite long periods of hospitalization, Judy obtained her Masters degree in Education, and taught two years before a bone infection finally took her life September 1974. Over the course of her illness, friends and family never stopped praying for her. Every time Judy faced another crisis, prayer groups across the city and beyond were formed—and for a time, she would miraculously rally. My dad, a staunch believer in the healing power of prayer, truly believed she could be healed if our faith was strong enough. When he finally realized we were going to lose her, in spite of his faith, he was devastated.

Her funeral should have been a glorious celebration of her young life and her accomplishments—of her beauty, her talents, and her spirit—with the deep realization that she was now free from suffering. Yet, there was no joy or peace in our collective sorrow; maybe for some, but certainly not for me. Instead, a heavy pall of grief seemed to pervade the air, so strong among family and peers it felt palpable. Why—because we had glimpsed a great potential in her. Just twenty-eight years old, our grief was for a life not lived to its fullest, taken before she had a chance to live it.

My husband, not understanding my deep feelings for a beautiful life taken before its prime, kept reminding me of how much she had suffered and how I should be glad she no longer had to endure such pain. Notwithstanding that this logic made perfect sense, it did nothing to heal a deeper wound in my heart. Grief cannot be logically rationalized or explained away. Its roots lie too deep in the realm of the subconscious—in the mystery and fear of death itself.

Nor could that same logic heal the wound in my father's heart. Two years later, at age seventy-eight, he died of congestive heart failure. After Judy's death, he visited her grave two or three times a week. On his last day he visited the cemetery, tended his roses, bathed, and ate lunch before relaxing in his easy chair to await a World Series game. He dosed off peacefully and never awoke.

* * *

What was so remarkable about his funeral in comparison to Judy's was an overwhelming, pervading sense of peace for a long life, well lived. He was often heard to say, (speaking to God) "I'm ready when you are;" therefore, releasing him into that heavenly kingdom didn't carry the same shock and trauma as letting Judy go.

Still, losing him was another deep psychological shock that set in motion the natural grieving process again.

* * *

One of my earliest experiences, while visiting relatives one summer, was witnessing their grief over the death of their beloved dog. Never having had a pet, I couldn't really relate to the grief my cousins were expressing. My mother felt the loss of a pet was reason enough not to own one. Still, I wanted our children to have the experience of pets. When they were little we had the usual array of Easter bunnies, a hamster, a parakeet and budgie, and two darling kittens, brother and sister. Losing them was not the same trauma as when we lost our beloved, beautiful Irish setter, Julie. We had acquired her in England as a puppy and from the beginning she let us know her sole purpose in life was to love each one of us unconditionally. We took her on our walks and family outings, but it was C.B. and the children who spent extra time petting and grooming her. I was too busy with other things to give her special time and attention.

Julie was eight years old when our youngest left home for college. About eleven o'clock one evening, without prior warning of any trouble, we heard her moans outside our window. A hurried trip to our veterinarian's clinic couldn't save her. My immediate reaction to her sudden death was mixed. My heart, full of love and appreciation for her devotion to our family, was coupled with guilt and remorse for not having given her more time and affection. In the wee morning hours, as I tried to sleep, I saw her running toward me. When she leapt over a privet hedge and I could see her body through the hedge I realized she was appearing to me as a transparent spirit. Through my tears I felt her lick my face as if to say, "Don't cry. I love you and forgive you." This was a very profound experience—like none I had had before or have had since.

* * *

If I had been able to share my fears of death and dying with my parents as a child, perhaps I would have lost some of the fear and mystery of death. Was this a problem for other families? What my family, and many others as well, needed was the services of an organization not yet founded—known today as "Hospice." This volunteer program was designed specifically for terminally ill patients and their families, with highly qualified personnel trained to provide all manner of care and services to patients and their family.

These volunteers, adept at listening and encouraging dialogue among family members, provide a support system that enables the family to find closure and comfort in the last days. Such a support system would have encouraged our family to talk openly about death, to deal with our feelings of losing a loved one, and to better understand the grieving process. Such a service would have been great solace for Judy in her last days and to our family—enabling us to say "I love you" and "Goodbye."

* * *

In the '80s I took a class on 'Death and Dying' at our Science of Mind Church in Seattle. One of our assignments was, "If we knew we only had six months or a year to live, how would we wish to live those last months?" This was not something I had thought much about; nor was it a subject I relished thinking about at the time. Nonetheless, it seemed a good exercise. I thought of an early dream of wanting to see the world. Some part of me would love to kick back and travel abroad—experiencing the rich and varied cultures of the world. Another part felt a strong commitment to finish the work I had started a few years earlier—to complete my spiritual memoirs. Somehow I felt my soul's destiny lay in sharing my truth, not only as I was living it, but also through the written word.

Little did I know how many years would transpire before this book would be finished!

Chapter 20

"For God hath not given us a spirit of fear,
but of power, and of love, and of a sound mind."
2 Tim. 1-7

The impact of that workshop with Dr. Joy in the fall of 1988—followed that December by the year-end Asilomar retreat—then the death of my mother the following spring—led me to wonder what would be coming up next in my life. I had requested Dr. Joy's conference calendar, and, as soon as it arrived, my question was answered. The Foundational conference was scheduled for November 1989, and I knew I would be there.

With this decision, I realized I would again be stepping off into unknown and uncharted waters—but the dye had been cast. The material I had been introduced to earlier, in Seattle and Asilomar, was so rich I wanted to explore it for further insights. When I indicated a desire to enroll in this Conference, Brugh was careful to point out that "this level of work was not without risks, for who knows what the psyche will reveal that we may not be prepared to handle." From my ordinary sense of self, I felt apprehensive about what this might entail, especially since I had little knowledge of this aspect of the human mind. Still, despite his warning and some misgivings, from a deeper place within me, I was ready.

After almost twenty fulfilling years in the Science of Mind—as student, teacher, and licensed practitioner—I had gained some understanding of the Universal principles we are meant to live by, and had been healed in mind and spirit in many wonderful ways. Yet there was no denying that my body was decidedly out of balance. At first I thought this imbalance was related to rheumatoid arthritis, which, of course, it was. Now I wondered if this imbalance could also be related to focusing practically all of my time and attention seeking after mental and spiritual understanding, without giving proper time and attention to my human needs.

My earlier prayers had been to heal this imbalance. That amazing dream/vision in 1987* had been a powerful message, indicating I would leave one teaching for another. Indeed, I felt I was guided to this new teaching as I had been to the Science of Mind teachings. With the knowledge I had gleaned from my years in Science of Mind, as well as my early exposure to the *Holy Bible* and the teachings of Jesus, I believed I was prepared for this next step. Those teachings had been an answer to years of longing for some measure of understanding.

Now, Dr. Joy's conference work would engage, not the conscious mind, but those unconscious forces that operate below the conscious mind. I was excited about this new adventure and grateful to have Dr. Joy as my guide. ** By this time, Brugh had been facilitating these conferences in the field of 'energy medicine' for some fifteen years and had become well known here and abroad. In his book, *Joy's Way,* he had given a description of the energy centers in the body and their particular function. I learned there were seven major centers, called chakras in the Eastern tradition—the root chakra at the base of the spine, the sexual chakra located just below the navel, the solar plexus chakra over the diaphragm, the heart chakra, the throat chakra, the third eye chakra located between the eyes, and the crown chakra at the top of the head. Above that, was an eighth chakra—called the transpersonal. We learned that each center played a specific role in the well being of an individual. For optimum health, each chakra not only needed to be harmonized and balanced within itself, but in harmony with all the other centers as well.

As for myself I had heard the word "chakra" before, but had paid little heed. After all, this was a foreign word not readily admis-

* Chapter 16
** Appendix A (Brief bio.)

sible to my western mind. Unaware that these energy centers even existed (by whatever name), I was completely ignorant that they existed as a vital life force within me. I had no idea where they fit into the totality of my being. Perhaps the imbalances in my body were the result of some of these centers not performing as they were meant to perform. Hopefully, this conference would answer that question.

Brugh believes the heart center/chakra is a transcendent place where we can actually achieve a state of consciousness above judgments of good and bad—where we can see those aspects of the deep psyche that have, heretofore, been hidden from our awareness.

He deduced that "Only this heart center had the capacity to love, forgive, heal, and redeem those unlovely and unloving parts of our psyche. Only from *this* center are we able to look with loving compassion at those acrimonious parts of ourselves, to acknowledge and accept them and give them a place to speak. Only from our heart center are we able to gather each one in our arms and become the Good Samaritan to them."

* * *

We arrived for this Foundational conference the morning of November 20, 1989 in varying states of anticipation and trepidation. Some arrived by car, but most flew into Paulden, Arizona from points beyond, where vans met and drove us another twenty-five minutes to The Conference Center. My first impression of the facility, as it came into view, was of one rather large imposing structure surrounded by a grouping of smaller buildings—all constructed of rough dark-stained wood, befitting this high desert area. This larger building, stood behind and above the others—affording a panoramic view to the south from large wrap-around picture windows and a surrounding deck. No doubt this was where our sessions would take place.

We were met by Brugh and his staff and given a schedule of daily activities, some general rules and guidelines, and a roster of all those attending. Then we were assisted with our luggage to our assigned quarters. I noted the schedule each day would begin with early morning meditation; then four people would be initiated through a formal ritual into their heart center. Following that would be dream work with Brugh—breakfast—and then another session with Brugh until lunchtime. Afternoons were free to explore as we chose until four o'clock when sessions would resume for the heart centering initiation of two more individuals—then dinner and an evening session. Our first session with Brugh would begin after dinner that evening.

As I stepped inside the foyer for the first time I was awed by two exquisite paintings by Gloria Joy, (Brugh's ex-sister-in-law) depicting the goddess emerging within the human figure. At the top of the stairs stood an enormous 'Laughing Buddha' to greet us—beautifully carved from rich wood. Entering the large meeting room through double doors, I was moved by a sense of the sacred. I knew Brugh had been instrumental in planning this facility—and it was especially evident in this spacious octagonal-shaped room.

A large stone fireplace surrounded by large picture windows, providing a magnificent view of the Chino Valley. The deep plush mauve carpet was vacuumed into a beautiful central design. Floor cushions with backrests were arranged in a large circle. Strategically placed around the perimeter, were several elaborately carved chests where sacred symbols from every religious discipline were displayed. I would soon become aware of another outstanding feature of this room—its first class hi-fidelity sound system.

* * *

An eclectic group of people had gathered—thirty in all, evenly divided between men and women. The session began with introductions, at which time my thoughts and impressions were very revealing. First, I observed a definite generation gap—with most participants my junior by fifteen or twenty years—with only two or three nearer my age. Moreover, the gap appeared to widen as we shared briefly something about ourselves, our life's work, and our reasons for being here.

Some participants had come from as far away as Montevideo, Uruguay; Edinburgh, Scotland; and Victoria, B.C., Canada. The rest of us were from scattered regions within the United States. Judging the poise and self-assurance of many of these individuals, my assessment was that most were quite successful in their chosen careers. I also sensed that some were already well schooled in these teachings, and more psychically-attuned and spiritually-mature than I.

The issue was not so much my judgment of these people as it was my judgment of self in comparison. This caused me to feel decidedly out of my element, and for several days I felt very much the introvert bumping up against all these gregarious extroverts. As the week progressed and people began to share their major challenges and, for some, life threatening issues, I began to feel more relaxed, more at one with the group, and definitely more compassionate.

* * *

Too late I remembered the three injunctions Dr. Joy had given for this level of work in his book, *Joy's Way*; "#1—make no comparisons; #2—make no judgments; #3—delete your <u>need</u> to understand." As a Religious Science practitioner I had diligently sought not only to follow these precepts in my daily life, but especially in my role as a practitioner. They were, in fact, considered an integral part of the healing consciousness. Here, in a completely new and different environment, I had inadvertently fallen into an earlier pattern of making comparisons and judgments. How had this happened?

I thought I had learned to transcend that mode of comparing and judging myself with others—operating now from another, more accepting mode of thinking and being. Yet, in an instant, I had unconsciously slipped back into an old pattern of self-judgment. Not a happy place to be! The lesson learned from this experience was that this negative pattern was still with me. Regrettably, this was a hard truth I thought I had previously learned from Ernest Holmes, when he said that our old habits keep returning. Those old 'habits' were seen by Brugh as unconscious 'patterns' that will always be with each one of us because they are a part of who and what we are as human beings. But, as Brugh said, "*they are only one part.*" I hoped there were more resourceful parts as well.

* * *

That first evening Brugh said that, "*at unconscious levels* we are multi-dimensional. Not only are we multi-dimensional but we operate from many states of consciousness, often simultaneously, without knowing this about ourselves." He had mentioned this before; still the scope of such a concept was hard to fathom. I had earlier encountered in myself opposing points of view regarding certain issues, specifically my early religious beliefs versus a new revelation of Spirit. Did this term "multi-dimensional" explain those conflicting voices within me?

Brugh pointed out that "we are polarities of light and shadow—projecting onto others that which we deny in ourselves, not realizing that *what we see and judge as being outside ourselves is, in reality, within us.*" I was familiar with these terms, but only as a mental concept. Now they were being presented, *not as theoretical ideas, but as real aspects* of my unconscious mind. Are we, as Brugh says, "many selves inside, moving from part to part, unconsciously and automatically, when circumstances dictate?"

Considerable time was spent in our daily dream sessions, interpreting and detailing individual dreams. One morning while working with a dreamer (pointing out to us an example of our multi-dimensional nature) in response to a question he had asked, he heard, i*n just one sentence,* these shifts in consciousness—first, the innocent child (who doesn't know), then the victim (who blames others), and finally an adult (willing and able to take responsibility.)

* * *

In our orientation that first evening, we were informed that our sessions would always begin with the heart centering exercise, not only to anchor our consciousness there, but also to establish this exercise as a daily habit for all our inner work. Only from the heart center were we to approach the hidden nature of the unconscious. Our work would include working with dreams, hi-intensity sound, journaling, drawing, and contemplative walks in the desert.

We were encouraged to record our dreams and bring them to our session each morning where Brugh would select one or two each day to interpret. I wondered if I would wake up and recall enough of a dream to write it down. I had had no trouble waking and remembering those amazing dreams I share in this book; however, they appeared to be of a different order than my ordinary dreams. Years ago I had made a concerted effort to remember and record my dreams. At one point I was waking up often during the night to write them down. The end result was a lack of sleep and fatigue the following day. It wasn't long before I slipped back into not waking at all. For this conference I hoped I would awaken and remember a dream.

* * *

Also, in our orientation we were reminded to watch our step and be alert to the wildlife native to this area. This national forest was home to the deadly Mohave rattler, as well as scorpions, mountain lions, coyotes, and a host of smaller more benign creatures. My initial observation earlier that day was that, except for a few bird calls, the place seemed strangely silent. Many desert plants and trees appeared in various stages of distress—some dying or dead. We were told that there had been no rain here in over a year! Unfamiliar with nature as pristine as this, never having hiked with others or alone in a wilderness area, I was suddenly aware of how dangerous this place was for a tenderfoot. Nonetheless, Brugh encouraged us to explore our surroundings on our own. Those first ventures were timid at best and layered with fears of surprising some predator on my path.

The time for courage, faith, and trust necessary for this level of work had arrived, but I hadn't guessed it would also include facing down my fears of taking solitary walks in a wilderness setting. Still, I had come to this remote area far from the noise and pollution of suburbia for spiritual growth and healing. Indeed, there was something awesome about putting aside normal everyday activities and family responsibilities for the sake of exploring more deeply one's inner life. I felt privileged to be here in such a unique place.

Brugh called his conference work "mystery training" for good reason; it was far beyond the body of knowledge understood and accepted by Western society and traditional religious institutions. For eons, these teachings have remained hidden from the vast majority of people because of the grave danger of entering these studies too soon or with wrongful intent. For this level of work one must be prepared and willing to take on the responsibility of using the power and wisdom contained therein—not only wisely, but also lovingly—which means *for the greater good of humanity.* Otherwise, we can do great harm to ourselves and others. The message is clear: *"The ego cannot be in charge!"* A fully qualified teacher is required to lead the student safely through the reefs and shoals of the deep psyche.

Although I was apprehensive that this conference would reveal things about me that I really didn't want to see, at the same time, I considered that further healing might lie in such a revelation. From my reactions to the people I met that first evening, and my cautious forays into the desert, I was already learning important truths about myself. Brugh's premise, that "we must bring to consciousness that which is working against our best interests in order to be made whole," meant the need to see and accept those parts of ourselves we'd rather not acknowledge as belonging to us.

Having already encountered information that seriously challenged my ego sense of self, I was reminded of what Brugh had written in his book, *Joy's Way:* "The ego, or conscious mind, is 99.9999% comatose, while the knowledge and wisdom we seek lies in other areas that can only be accessed through quiet contemplation and the surrender of ego." During our three day fasting this coming weekend, there would be time to reflect on these lessons in self-discovery—from the many new and startling bits of information I had received so far.

Chapter 21

"To get at the core of God at His greatest,
one must first get into the core of himself at his least,
for no one can know God who has not first known himself."
Meister Eckhart, a 13th century Dominican monk and Christian mystic

This two-week Foundational Conference was an introduction into "the feminine mysteries." The purpose was to initiate a pathway into the deeper realms of mind/body/soul/spirit through dream work, and other modalities. We would also be initiated individually into our heart center in a formal, sacred ceremony. In the earlier workshop with Brugh, I was introduced to the transcendent qualities of the heart center. I had been focusing on those qualities of deep compassion, unconditional love, innate harmony, and a sense of a holy Presence in my meditations. For that reason I was pleased to be one of the first to be initiated the second morning of the conference.

For our initiation, four of us were dressed in white. The meeting room had been prepared with four tables positioned to face north, south, east, and west. Everyone had been given an assigned role, either as the ones being initiated, standing with others beside an initiate at the table, or sitting in silence in a circle surrounding the four tables. Sacred music set the stage for this most solemn ceremony. Through the power and inspiration of his words, Brugh deftly guided us through the proceedings, inducting each of us in turn into our heart center. I was summarily impressed by his attention to every detail and how smoothly everything went. I was so appreciative of the opportunity to receive such a blessed gift.

I prayed to surrender and trust this initiatory process for I believed deeply that "A force beyond my conscious knowing," (meaning Spirit) was in charge of my being here. Thinking I was fully open and accepting of this initiation I must have been pretty much shut down on some level. I had expected some wonderful euphoric feeling, some joyful elation, perhaps a slight indication in my heart area from this experience. This was not forthcoming. I was surprised and disappointed that I felt so little of the loving, healing energy being bestowed upon me.

Remembering something Brugh had said earlier about our hi-intensity exercises, that even if one falls asleep "something is still taking place *energetically.*" I hoped "Something true and deep" had touched me in this ritual to stir and awaken my heart center. Having had a direct experience of Spirit years ago, I thought of myself as spiritually oriented, but it had taken this heart initiation to reveal the full extent to which I was disconnected from my body and my feeling nature.

During these two weeks—in different scenarios and with varying reactions—I would meet, again and again, hidden aspects of my psyche. According to Brugh:

> "To explore the deep psyche and bring to our awareness that which needs healing in ourselves requires losing our innocence. We must go within and silence the negative voices of fear, and surrender our pettiness and our littleness to a higher, nobler part. If we are to accomplish great things, we must somehow find and develop a faith and belief in our inherent goodness."

That was what this conference was about; it was what I sought. At the same time, I had no idea what other issues would surface. Along with some anxiety, there was also an excitement at what might be revealed! Very much aware that we were dealing with material considered "verboten" by conventional wisdom (meaning traditional Christian religion and Western society) I, nonetheless, meant to press ahead to discover who I was at deeper levels. To allow that to happen meant surrendering and trusting Spirit—and surrendering meant giving up control!

One reason I had been so pleased to find the philosophy of Science of Mind was that, at the time, it gave me some much needed control over my mental, emotional, and spiritual life. Science of Mind had also given me tools with which to structure my thoughts and words in a positive, healthy way, enabling me to consciously begin to change those beliefs that no longer fit my new understanding and experience of God. Ernest Holmes's writings had expanded my concept of God as divine Mind and Spirit and given me a deep faith in the power of prayer. In that teaching I also discovered that when I aligned myself with the Spirit of God's Love and asked for a healing or a blessing, "in faith believing," a reciprocal action followed. The only name I could give it was "grace."

* * *

In this conference, each exercise was designed to put us in touch with our intuitive feeling nature—perhaps to catch a glimpse of what needed to be healed and integrated. Leading us in all of our various activities, Brugh gave us only a few instructions so that we could go in and experience for ourselves what might be revealed. The morning he handed each of us a Tarot deck a bright red flag went up for me! I had heard some scary things about Tarot cards and the power they held. A friend once told me about a mutual acquaintance who, after spending some time working with the Tarot, ended up in the psychiatric ward in our local hospital. I also knew that the Tarot was considered by many Christians the work of the Devil.

However, when I was told that the Tarot was a mirror to the unconscious I realized I would have to work through my fears regarding it. I felt somewhat relieved when I heard that Anthropologist Margaret Mead, whose work I admired, had found the Tarot valuable in her work. Nonetheless, I opened my deck with some trepidation. Voicing my fears, I was told to hold the deck reverently and ask permission before seeking to use it, which I did. The first answer was a definite "No," whereupon I put them aside and entered a quiet meditative state. When I asked the second time I was given permission. (Evidently one must be in the proper state of mind to work with the wisdom of the Tarot.) On first examination I saw that each card was a complexity of symbols beyond my capacity to comprehend. From my reasoning, rational, left-brain mind I could make no sense of them at all.

As a way to familiarize ourselves with the cards we were asked to select the card we most liked and the one we most disliked. This took ten or fifteen minutes—shuffling through our decks studying each card. We were then asked to look for the positive aspects in the card we most disliked and for negative aspects in the card we liked the most. This exercise forced me to look more deeply for subtle, abstract clues. As I studied the symbols in the card I most liked I saw they reflected the dream/vision I had had in August 1987.

The card was the Ace of Cups and its positive aspects pictured a gigantic hand of some Super-being appearing out of the clouds, offering a cup overflowing with the waters of life. Contained also in the cup was a golden egg (which I thought might be the pearl of great price/or seed of truth) and hovering over and behind it was the symbol of peace, or divine blessing for the planet. The card was well balanced, containing all the elements of earth, fire, air, and water. After a long search for the negative aspect of this card someone pointed out the absence of a human figure—all the symbols were cosmic and abstract.

The card I most disliked was the Ten (X) of Swords and no wonder. Here was a picture of a head and upper torso lying face down on what looked like a blanket of snow. Ten swords penetrated the body from the neck, both shoulders, three in the upper back, two mid-back, one at the waist and one just below the waist. The head and chest area were bathed in a pool of blood. The negative aspects of this card signified cold, cut off from the warmth of the sun —and death and dying, the loss of life energy. Also, the figure was pinned down and immobilized by ten swords of equal size and power. I could see nothing positive about this card.

Fortunately, several people familiar with the Tarot came to my rescue by observing that the swords, being double-edged, might contain new life that comes with death to an old way of living one's life. Also snow, the symbol of purity, surrounded the perimeter of the body and the blood was contained within that perimeter. There was not a sword through the heart therefore the figure may not have been mortally wounded. This could symbolize the death of the ego. These interpretations gave me much to ponder.

* * *

Practicing our heart-centering meditation more deeply, focusing on our heart energy field as an artesian well, visualizing a radiant ball of light moving out of our heart into our body, and out into our arms and hands activated the process. In a giving mode, placing our hands on our heart, we were to *feel our hands radiating this ball of light into our heart center.* Then moving to the receiving part of our psyche, we were to *feel this radiant light entering our heart center.* In this exercise we became aware that giving and receiving energy were not the same.

Several days were allotted to practicing this heart-centering exercise with different partners. In these sessions we practiced moving the energy from our heart into our hands and into the heart of our partner—then experiencing, from our partner, the energy coming into our heart from his/her hands. I was amazed the first time I placed my palms together, without touching, and felt a tingling of energy between them. Even though I had felt that initial movement of energy between my palms, I wasn't yet able to feel this energy moving up and out of my heart into my hands, much less into the heart area of my partner.

I had the same difficulty shifting my focus from a giving mode to a receiving mode—feeling this energy coming into my heart center from my partner. Nonetheless, I held the intention that subtle energies were being set in motion on a deep level and a pathway was being established. Some members of the group were healers, familiar with these healing energies, but, as a novice, I needed practice, practice, practice—just to get to the feeling stage.

Brugh held the belief that when we acknowledge and appreciate our physical body, we are building a bridge back into our body, which will then respond. The practice of moving this heart energy through the body seemed a perfect way to heal the split between mind and spirit, and body and soul.

* * *

Each morning Brugh would select someone's dream from a basket. His intention was to draw from the dreamer not only their initial impressions and feelings about their dream but, more importantly, to engage the dreamer in exploring the hidden meaning behind the symbols. We were informed that the deep psyche doesn't care about specifics; it reads patterns; mother energies, father energies, male/female energetics, curved lines, angular lines, and color. By far, the biggest shock for me was to learn that the psyche reveals our psychological material through basic sexual symbols. For instance, any elongated object is seen by the psyche as a masculine image or phallus, while a round or deep image is seen as a womb or vagina.

This reduction to basics enables one to see more clearly the underlying psychological pattern being played out in the dream, simply because their meaning cannot be understood from a conscious, rational viewpoint. To understand and interpret dreams, we must learn to read them from a pattern level. My question was, how does one reach that "pattern-level" state of mind? What was the pattern in the dream I had the first night of the conference?

The dream: I was on a train and had locked myself inside a pristine stainless steel restroom when I sensed someone trying to open the door. I quickly rechecked the lock to make sure it was secured. There the dream ended.

Brugh's interpretation was a revelation. The train was a masculine symbol—the restroom was the feminine symbol. I was told my description of this restroom as stainless steel and pristine was indicative of some beliefs and attitudes I hold about my own sexuality. The fact that I kept this door securely locked made clear my intention to keep this part of my psyche off limits. I felt threatened by the knock on the door and what might be revealed if I opened it. The dream was showing me my fears about opening to inquiry and exploration. Who was knocking at the door? No doubt it was Brugh. With his ability to read patterns, I was making doubly sure he was locked out!

* * *

I learned that the classic pattern I carry is one many men and women carry—that is, to view the feminine nature as weak (implying inferior) and the masculine as strong (with the connation of being superior.) This pattern was not, as I had thought, simply a collective worldview outwardly imposed upon women by society and religion, but one also inherited from our ancestors and encoded in our genes. The masculine aspect of our psyche is the linear, logical, reasoning, conscious mind. Our feminine nature is the intuitive, nurturing, creative, unconscious mind. I had honored the one and put down the other.

I believe the Western mind-set—focused as it is on the physical and sexual differences between men and women and on the reality of the physical world—have placed an over-emphasis on logical, rational thinking as superior to the creative, intuitive, unconscious aspects of who and what we are. As a result, we have failed to see that both men and women carry the basic elements of these masculine and feminine energies in their psyches. I'm not referring here to sexual orientation but rather to our psychological makeup. According to Brugh, a recognition and appreciation of both masculine and feminine qualities within oneself can begin to heal this split.

* * *

During one of our hi-intensity sound exercise I was presented with a vivid image symbolic of my "classic pattern." The music was the Overture from Tannhauser, in two parts. In the first movement I saw myself as an eagle, soaring high and free above a beautiful canyon. The eagle did not enter the canyon to look for prey but stayed high aloft. Even though I knew the eagle must fly down into the canyon from time to time in search of food, I identified myself with its freedom of flight rather than a bird of prey. Commenting on this image later Brugh pointed out that the eagle, being non-human, was something of a "non-compute" for him. Still, an eagle was decidedly a masculine image. Whatever was in that canyon (the canyon being a feminine symbol) was vulnerable to the strength and power of this masculine image. Therefore, the "feminine" dared not show itself for fear of its very life.

In the second movement I had an entirely different experience. I saw myself donning plated armor in preparation to enter the caverns of my psyche to fight the "dragon." However, as I approached the entrance to the dragon's cave I was suddenly overcome with deep compassion and unconditional love for this creature—and in that moment the need to fight the dragon dissolved. Both of these visions provided invaluable material for further study.

* * *

At each turn, I learned something new about myself—through my observations and interactions with other participants—from my introduction to the Tarot and I Ching—from my dreams—from those hi-intensity images—from hiking on the desert trail—and from our three days of silence and fasting. Many of the feelings, thoughts, images, and emotions that came forward in these two weeks were not my strengths and capabilities; rather there was a growing awareness of my weaknesses and inadequacies. I wondered if this was the catharsis needed to get past my ego and my defenses to allow the activation of my heart center.

* * *

Our closing ceremony was magnificently choreographed. Brugh rehearsed our entrance that afternoon so that we would know what to expect and the proceedings would flow smoothly. Later he transformed the room into a sacred temple with special lighting, sacred music, and a profusion of flowers. Dressed in white and carrying bouquets of flowers, we entered single file at the appointed hour, forming a circle around the room. Brugh led us through a beautiful and deeply-moving ritual to honor the forces that had come forward during the conference to bless each of us with insights and wisdom. And then it was over.

After breakfast the following morning we said our informal goodbyes in this very versatile room where all of our work had taken place. It was no longer the sacred temple of the night before, but again a working model for healing and transformation.

PART III:

SYNTHESIS INTO WHOLENESS

Epigram:
"It is only with the heart that we can see rightly;
What is essential is invisible to the eye."
Antoine de Saint-Exupery

Chapter 22

"He that findeth his life shall lose it;
and he that loseth his life for my sake
shall find it.
Matt. 10:39

Entitled "Intuitive Awakening," my next conference with Brugh—scheduled for November 17-29, 1990—would be an initiation into the 5th and 6th energy fields—also known as the Throat and the Third Eye Chakras. We would meet again at the same retreat center in Arizona. This gave me a year to work with the heart centering meditation in preparation.

A letter from Brugh, a month prior to the conference, reminded us, "as we move beyond the Heart Center we should be aware of the consequences of opening more expanded levels of intuitional awareness, and the necessity of being objective and staying centered in "a non-egotistic place." It is not the general shadow content of the unconscious that can disrupt the developing individual (although uncomfortable material can appear at any level of study.) Rather, it is the seduction into power and the misuse of power that can impede the opening of these states, or actually injure the soul's development if not handled appropriately."

> His instructions were to begin two weeks prior to the conference to set our intention, in daily meditation, to allow the natural unfoldment of the 5th and 6th Chakras, and to request, in our dreams and meditations, guidance and

> support from the unconscious parts of ourselves. Curious about the characteristics of the chakras, I found a book by Jack Schwartz, titled *Human Energy Systems*, that described these charkas in depth. Basically, they were identified by their color and type. Initiations into these particular chakra centers were essential for the development of intuitive awareness and spiritual growth.

* * *

In Religious Science, the approach to Spirit is through the conscious mind. In these conferences with Brugh I was being shown another perspective—"that no matter how 'enlightened' we think we are in our conscious understanding of 'what is,' there are unconscious forces at work beyond our knowing and control."

From years of conference work, Brugh found that difficult and/or destructive behavioral patterns could be healed and integrated if they were brought to our conscious awareness.

> Then—to quote Brugh—if we could honestly acknowledge, accept, and appreciate those lost and hurtful parts of ourselves as the complexity of who we are as human beings—"if these parts were given a place to speak"—the healing could commence. Intuitive soul development was "not *just* about discovering hidden aspects of our psyche and bringing them to consciousness for healing and renewal, and learning to access greater insights and wisdom contained in the unconscious, but through these avenues, we are brought into a wonderful sense of connection and harmony within ourselves and with God as well. Mind with body—body with soul—soul with spirit.

> According to Brugh—there are two great mysteries tied up in the feminine forces: 'intuitional awareness' and 'healing at an intrinsic innate level.' The key to *this* training is to understand yourself as an instrument of this wisdom where you *allow* these resources to come forward. This protects your ordinary senses from inflation."

* * *

The day I arrived my hopes were high, yet several days into the conference I wrote in my journal some disconcerting thoughts and feelings:

> I notice a recurrence of my basic patterning—discovered last year in my first conference with Brugh—of how I immediately take on a mental stance in defense against exposing my feeling nature. I notice this in how I respond in our group sessions, and in how I interact in social settings. From the start, my conscious intention has been to open to intimacy and to an easy dialogue with other participants. Instead, I am feeling an intense vulnerability and a growing sense of separation and isolation.
>
> But more than this, I am aware of other areas of discomfort. Not only am I having difficulty expressing my thoughts and feelings in both these arenas, I am also feeling a tightness in my throat. My hearing appears to have worsened, especially the ringing in my ears, and for several days now I have had difficulty hearing much of what has been said in our sessions. These symptoms may be an outpicturing of unconscious resistance and fear to whatever issues might be revealed in the coming days.

* * *

Brugh's focus was to move us beyond our objective, logical, conscious mind into deeper, subjective ranges of the unconscious for healing and integration, yet here I was—still playing out the pattern of running from my feminine, right-brain, unconscious feelings into the safety of my masculine, left brain, conscious intellect. No wonder I was feeling uncomfortable. (At least, I was getting in touch with my feelings!) I had to wonder though—if I was not prepared, committed, and willing to open to the intuitive resources of the Throat and Third Eye Chakras, why was I here? What did I have to fear in opening to these levels of consciousness?"

I wasn't sure, but one thought later came to mind—the danger Brugh had referred to earlier, of becoming 'ego-inflated' by the power of insights and revelations that would be forthcoming. My question to myself; "Was opening to the feminine side of my nature, with its deeper wisdom and power, a legitimate fear, or was this just another excuse to avoid taking adult responsibility for my life"? When Jesus made the statement that we must lose our life in order to find it, I believe he was talking about losing our little sense of self as we begin to realize our spiritual connection to God. Was I ready to surrender my little ego self and make that leap in consciousness?

Brugh's aim was to lead us to a place where we could read dreams from 'pattern level'—to see the playing and replaying of family patterns, generation after generation. Reading dreams from this level required a new way of perceiving and 'non-thinking' that, at this stage, was still quite beyond me. Unable to recognize family patterns in my ordinary dreams or in the symbols of the Tarot, I noticed some others were having the same problem. Were we afraid to look too closely at those images for what sinister aspects they might reveal? Perhaps I was!

I had to admire Brugh's patience. In every session and with each one of us—sometimes gently, sometimes not—he coaxed and cajoled us to recognize those unconscious patterns showing up over and over in our inner and outer lives. To him, these patterns were not only evident in our dreams—they could also be observed in our day-to-day <u>re</u>activity to certain people, places, and things—especially to our "hot button" issues. Awakening to these inner thoughts, feelings, core beliefs, dominant attitudes, and behavior could tell us much about ourselves on many levels.

* * *

We looked forward to the daily 'hi-intensity sound' exercises, designed to elicit vivid imagery of our patterns dancing in a dream-like state. Stretched out comfortably on the deep carpet of our conference room, we opened to the powerful vibrations of the selection for the day. Allowing the music to take us on a surreal journey into the unconscious, we each had an experience uniquely personal and relevant. Again, in the same manner as dreams, Brugh interpreted one or two of these experiences for us.

Daily we drew a Tarot card as our teacher for the day. Our intention was to gain some insight into what our unconscious might be seeking to reveal. At the same time, we were also exploring the mystery of the I Ching and the Runes, searching for more psychological clues as to what the unconscious patterns are that "drive" us. Deciphering the meaning of these mysterious symbols was for me like learning a foreign language. Still unable to interpret their meanings, others continued to help. Amazingly, their interpretations resonated with what I intuitively felt was true but could not define on my own.

* * *

Thankfully, as the work progressed, earlier symptoms faded and I began to hear things I couldn't hear before. Indeed, each day was a new revelation, with Brugh attuned to what needed to be addressed in each circumstance and with each person. His insight into my canyon dream the year before had opened my eyes to the truth that my feminine nature (symbolized by the canyon) was completely overshadowed by the powerful masculine symbol of an eagle soaring high above the canyon floor—posing an ever-present threat to the survival of the feminine should she show herself. As I mulled over this information I realized I had hardly progressed beyond a conscious recognition of this pattern.

Those vivid images revealed succinctly my classic pattern of seeing the masculine/mental side of my psyche as powerful and superior, while seeing my feminine/feeling nature as powerless and inferior. Psychologically, this was how I defended against my feelings of intense vulnerability. Seeing this pattern now as an arrested infantile development I could no longer afford, I made a firm commitment to accept and appreciate fully the attributes of both my masculine and feminine natures. Awakened to this pattern in my psyche, I felt I was ready to reclaim the power I had long ago given away.

Preparing for our initiation, we were asked to draw a Tarot card and pose the question, "What might be the obstruction to my upcoming initiation?" My first block, of course, was my inability to read the psychological symbols on the Tarot card I had drawn, much less find the meaning *behind* those images. I appreciated Brugh's comment that "although a shadow can be dark, it is not necessarily so. A shadow is simply that which we do not know about ourselves." This assuaged some fears about my shadow. When my partner offered his interpretation of my card—behold; his insight revealed yet another aspect to my classic pattern—a fear of surrendering conscious control of my life to a higher power.

Not only was I stuck in my left-brain, rational way of thinking; I also felt I was being held in check by my early religious background in my inability to fully appreciate and discern the wisdom of the Tarot. On the one hand, I was ready and willing to venture forth and trust the process. On the other hand, I was not. Stepping, as it were, into the deeper mysteries, I recognized how unprepared I felt. Fears of the ego being seduced by the power contained in these higher ranges of consciousness, or perhaps the temptation to misuse those powers, also loomed large in my mind.

There was also the realization that greater obligations and responsibilities would be required. All of these thoughts and feelings were more than enough to trigger strong physical and emotional responses. After all my work with Brugh, I couldn't believe I had come to a crossroad—of whether to leave the conference and these teachings, or stay. In an instant I knew I would stay. After all, I was here as an extension of my spiritual quest—to explore and touch basic aspects of my nature that had long been denied and shut down. I should have known, from my earlier battles, and from Brugh's comments, the pathway in would not be without hurdles.

Into my second week of this conference, I was still feeling very much the novice in terms of ignorance regarding this body of mystical knowledge—amazed at the depth and breadth of the unconscious. Brugh had reminded us often, that knowing truth from an intellectual standpoint, and feeling that truth as a direct experience, are two very different things. I had felt that truth from a direct experience of "Light/Energy" in 1972, and since then, in my prayer and meditation periods. I had come into these teachings with Brugh *knowing, at a deep spiritual level, this truth—that the only way to access the deeper regions of the soul was to actually enter into and feel a deeper experience.* I was here to redeem those lost and forsaken parts of myself in order to bring *balance and harmony* to my mind/body/soul/spirit—even if it might prove painful or scary.

* * *

Now that the heart centering meditation was becoming part of our daily routine, one day Brugh gave us a short affirmation into this state of consciousness. If we find ourselves in a difficult circumstance we can "*Pause—Center—and Shift*" into our heart center, and instantly have the resources needed to defuse a tense situation. This short "command-phrase" became a virtual 'Godsend' (no pun intended.) Had I been privy to this simple exercise years before, perhaps I would not have been caught in the chaos that ensued when my established beliefs were threatened by my new understanding of truth.

The truth in Brugh's statement that "the masculine (conscious mind) will always trample the feminine (the unconscious mind)," kept turning up during this conference. The rationale of my conscious mind repeatedly sought to undermine my faith and commitment to a teaching beyond its ability to comprehend. Sensing both an intense vulnerability, and also a major disconnect to these deeper parts of my psyche, the imperative of developing the heart center as my 'rock' became all too clear.

* * *

This conference was following basically the same format as the Foundational Conference. Through dream interpretations, hi-intensity sound exercises, the Tarot, and various other exercises we were further inducted into our soul nature. I looked forward to our three days of silence and fasting mid-way through the conference. This would give me further opportunities, not only to familiarize myself with the Tarot, the Chinese Book of Change—The "I Ching," and the Nordic Runes, but also time to enjoy my surroundings, to journal, enjoy the spa, sleep, read, rest, contemplate, and deepen.

The major work of this conference was, of course, our individual initiation into the Throat and Third-Eye Chakras.

> Brugh reminded us that what had been set in motion in our initiation ritual could not be called back. Moving out of the protection of childhood and its innocence into the richness of what it means to have maturation is the mystery of adulthood and the full power of incarnation. Now we face the mystery of the 'fall'—the mystery of potential rejection—the abandonment of others as they project onto us their hopes and their fears.

> When we begin to develop the heart center we gain a wonderful sense of well-being. Things will no longer hook us as we learn to prioritize what is important and what is not. Coming into a deeper place, we will have the capacity to live life more honestly and with greater courage. With the development of the heart center we are *fundamentally* changed inside.
>
> There are developmental sequences, breakthroughs, and transformations that can take place in these conferences at any time—not only immense leaps in consciousness, but also feelings of not having taken those leaps. How one celebrates the morning and allows life to dance is a major leap in one's development. Learning to appreciate—appreciate—appreciate is another major leap! Then, if there is some difficult thing we have to do we become aware of it and prepare for it. In the meantime, dreams reveal what's afoot.
>
> Once we become aware of these greater inner resources we no longer try to make key decisions from our conscious, thinking mind. We open to the intuitional. We become aware that we are simply a witness to a mystery beyond our conscious knowing—at which point we enter into the livingness of it—to redefine ourselves and enlarge our view of being.

In the months that followed, I continued to practice the heart centering exercises regularly, also recording some of my dreams. Following Inner Guidance, I began looking for patterns hidden in my dreams. Some months later the following poem came forward.

"Patterns Dancing."
Marvelous creatures, we humans;
And formidable, too.
Surface-conscious mostly. Of our
Depths – hardly a clue.
If we only knew!

Do we realize that our focus
Forms the boundary of our lives?
That the life we are experiencing
Comes from inner eye and mind?
If we looked, we'd find.

The people in my life
Aren't all they seem to be,
Mirroring reflections of
Deeper parts of me,
Parts I cannot see.

With each individual
I choose a certain stance,
Sometimes parent, sometimes child,
We dance a different dance.
Is this just happenstance?

Perhaps today a tyrant,
Tomorrow victimized.
Who is this mysterious stranger
Always in disguise?
Am I these many selves inside?

Are these inherent patterns
From a cosmic master plan:
And if brought to consciousness
Might we understand?
Wouldn't that be grand!

Chapter 23

"We were created to be in both the spiritual world
and the material world at the same time…
Our inner part is called our "spiritual self,"
because it is in heaven's light and our
outer self is called our "material self,"
because it is in the world's light."
From the theological writings of Emanuel Swedenborg

Through the centuries, although this truth has been reiterated again and again in the Scriptures—by the lives of Abraham, Moses, Jesus, Buddha, and Mohammed, as well as old and modern-day mystics in every culture—this truth has remained a secret hidden from view except to those who had "eyes to see and ears to hear." Jesus declared the truth that we live in two worlds; one—a physical/material universe of form, the other—a spiritual universe without physical form, and our task is find a way to "be in this *(physical/material)* world but not in it (*caught up in it.*)" (*My italics)* In my early years in the Science of Mind Church, a phrase I often heard was, "We are spiritual beings, living in a spiritual universe, having an earthly experience." Having encountered this spiritual world in my darkest hour, I knew it was true.

Now, Dr. Joy had given me tools to help integrate the split in my psyche between my mind/body/soul/spirit, and through the development of my heart center, a more direct approach to this spiritual dimension. No longer were my spiritual practices abstracted out of my body into my mind and spirit, but grounded in my body and soul as well. Continuing to engage my heart energy center, more fully appreciating the sacred qualities found there, I began to feel a closer connection in my body and soul to that of mind and spirit.

* * *

When Brugh's conference schedule for the next year arrived, I was pleased. A one-week 'Heart Deepening' Conference was being offered, back-to-back, with a one-week 'Call of the Ancestors' Conference, January 3-15, 1992—again in Arizona. The opportunity to deepen my heart center, as well as explore my family patterns, sounded interesting and valuable. Thinking of my larger family, those living and deceased, I felt both of these conferences would give me a chance to look more deeply into the family dynamics that had shaped me.

Saturday, December 28, 1991, seven days before the Heart Deepening Conference I had the following dream:

> I am in a large, white, sterile room—evidently in a medical facility. I see a very frail old man suffering from liver cancer lying on the lower shelf of a hospital gurney. I kneel down on his left side and place both my hands on his upper body. I say to him, "I have healing hands." Other women appear and do likewise and I add, "We all have healing hands." I see a glass jar filled with checks and money for him. I place a check for $25.00 in the jar. I feel deep compassion. The dream ends.

A few days into the conference I had some initial insights into the dream. On a personal level this dream seemed to indicate a serious illness or pending death of a man—maybe a male relative—to an ailment traditional medicine could not cure. My sense was that this dream was not a physical death but a psychological dying of some kind. The hospital staff appeared not to see this man. I, and other women who could see him, knelt and ministered "a healing touch."

From a collective viewpoint I thought the women kneeling beside me were symbolic of a new order coming forward, not to replace traditional medicine, but to work in conjunction with it. The message seemed clear, that true healing lies in the unconscious feminine energies—a truth not yet recognized by traditional medicine nor scientifically explained, understood, or accepted by society. Perhaps the collective unconscious was bringing forward an influx of feminine energies for healing and transformation.

My participation in this "laying on of hands" seemed a personal message that I might also be a healer. I didn't know what the jar and the $25.00 check meant, but my feelings of deep compassion suggested the heart level was somehow involved. Dreams are many-layered and can be seen from different perspectives, depending on one's intuitive development. I hoped to share this dream with Brugh sometime later in the week for his in-depth reading.

* * *

Opening the Conference that evening with a wonderful attunement to the heart center,

> Brugh reminded us again that—when our heart center is established, our life will begin to move out of fate into the courage to take on our destiny, and that of our family clan. However, coming into the heart center requires a death and transformation—and this is hard-won. A major, major transformation is the death of the ego!
>
> With the development of our heart center, the energy of crisis moves us from an infantile reactivity into a place that actually transforms the energy. By facing our life patterns, we further our development by taking them on as an initiation into a larger context.
>
> We find the heart center, not a personal individual state of consciousness, but one that subordinates our surface consciousness to the transcendent. This tells us that we are "both a mortal process, and also a trans-ordinary process." At this stage we must dissolve our personal attachments and get bigger.

Later that evening my prayer was to feel more deeply the attributes of the heart center—of unconditional love, deep compassion, innate harmony, and the embrace of a healing Presence. My desire was not simply to accept and appreciate more of who I am at these deeper levels—but to feel more closely this holy Presence and hear more clearly it's wisdom. I wanted to surrender, not only my need to consciously control my life, but also to give up my expectations and open to my deeper intuitive nature, "under grace and in perfect ways."

In a previous conference, Brugh had pointed out one pattern I carry—that I am "in service to the father," meaning the "masculine temple." His observation was that I was more oriented to conceptual thinking than to intuitive awareness, and although there is a joy in that, there is also a suffering. Although he felt this was well and good, it did tend to cut off other possibilities and ranges available at deeper levels. "Although we sacrifice a lot to do that, we are not responsible for this dynamic." Aware of my natural tendency toward "conceptual thinking," I, nonetheless, realized the true healing power of those feminine qualities of forgiveness and surrender to Spirit.

* * *

Our daily schedule began with early morning meditations—followed by dream work, hi-intensity sound sessions, and other related exercises—each one pointing us inward; not just to look at the unconscious patterns dancing in, around, and through us—but, more importantly, to *feel* them dancing. When elaborating someone's dream or a hi-intensity sound experience, Brugh drew from a vast storehouse of knowledge and wisdom. Throughout these pages, with his permission, I have shared his wisdom, either paraphrasing him from my notes, or quoting him directly from conference tapes.

> Continuing Brugh's comments: "Studies show that 70% (or perhaps more) of who we are lies in the unconscious and is not at choice. At unconscious levels each generation appears to live out the unresolved patterns of their parents, yet our destiny is not entirely personal. Most of our life is collective and we are involved in a collective destiny as well.

At this particular time in history we are witnessing the 'Collective Unconscious' as stirring and unstable—undergoing immense changes. ***Of all the time periods to know our heart center is now!*** *(Brugh's emphasis.)*

The world is transforming and each of us has a part to play in that transformation. This is a time where we can offer up our resources in service to a larger whole. Indeed, we are connected to something larger and our development is not just a personal, self-centered, selfish process.

By passing through the necessary initiations we contribute and give back to life from a larger, richer, deeper place. We open not only to our family destiny and to our personal soul destiny, but to the needs of the larger "collective" as well. Our greater task is to serve and nurture others as we nurture ourselves."

At one point Brugh was speaking of paradoxes and the fact that life cannot be all positive. I didn't want to hear it, but I knew it was true. I knew it from my own suffering that fateful day in 1972 when the pain became so great there was nothing left but surrender. In that surrender was an ecstasy so incredibly powerful and loving, my life was never again the same. I saw then that pain and ecstasy were paradoxically linked.

I awoke to a truth that one cannot experience a joyous breakthrough without first suffering a loss of some kind—"a paradoxical journey of stripping away all that would hinder the soul's progress."

From Brugh: As you deepen and mature you realize that in order to express yourself you speak in paradoxes. You speak of the elation and the pain, the agony and the ecstasy—the difficulties and the wonderment.

Here in this conference we are experiencing the paradox of being centered and vulnerable at the same time. It is through our vulnerability that the unconscious showers us with its resources. The minute we move to our strengths and our defenses, we cut off these amazing resources.

* * *

Later that week I shared my dream with Brugh who neatly bypassed my surface interpretation to give a much deeper, more intimate and revealing reading. He said, "In dream work body-parts represent patterns. What is killing off the masculine is a conflict of forces—of disowned material. The liver filters and detoxifies. It is a huge storage area for energy. (Liver—the word in living.) On the second shelf—this material is shelved—tucked away." He felt the dream wasn't about my own death but about something dying that was important to me.

Continuing his analysis, he felt that my confrontation was with God as Father figure—having disowned the split of a loving and judgmental God. "Psychologically, I hadn't known what to do with the darker force of the Father figure and also with the loving part." Likewise, he felt that arthritis in my body reflected this unresolved vengeance and righteousness of the Old God in conflict with the outer mind of a loving God. This disease reflected my inability to express this conflict in a healthy constructive way—causing tension in my hands and joints. He thought my unconscious feelings of rage and anger had never been allowed to express. "Arthritis is a self-destructive energy where one is usually afraid to express rage at the actual object."

I listened with arms crossed over my abdomen as Brugh gave these insights into my dream. In the past, every time Brugh tried to carry me into my shadow, I quickly moved out of it into "The Light." My body language caused him to finally ask, "Where are your feelings?" Having spent my life building defenses against expressing my feelings, being confronted now with this new information, I felt very vulnerable. Brugh felt there was a carcinoma going on, as revealed in the dream, that was really destroying a certain process, but to get to a realization I would first have to deal with all of the masculine overlays I use—where I leave my feelings and go into my head.

To Brugh, the dream indicated that the feminine energies realize the danger involved and are attempting to bring some sort of balanced healing to this area. Brugh felt there was something very important here if we could get through the mask I wear in my voice and demeanor. Speaking to me directly, he said, "When someone speaks with little or no feeling, the truth is that person is holding intense emotion underneath. Arthritis is an outward manifestation of the 'disconnect' from your feeling nature." He told me further, "You are not to deceive yourself by thinking you can integrate these issues from further insights. Intellectual insights are only the beginning of your development. At this stage of your life your richness and vitality lie in your feelings."

* * *

Later in the conference Brugh made the following statement that gave me much to ponder: "In broad general terms—there are only two things that lead to illness:

1) That we have lived too small a life for who and what we are—

2) Or more painfully, we have lived beyond who and what we are."

* * *

Further comments by Brugh at the close of this conference, discussing the challenges of the continued journey:

> As the deep psyche dances the mystery, we have to consciously put ourselves in accord with what the unconscious is developing. As the world goes into darkness the soul awakens (into the Light), and that is the Light we seek to guide us.
>
> The mystery of life is going to do to us what it needs to do, and our task is to somehow initiate through these major changes. If we regress, it is a failed initiation. The unconscious sees to it that none of us escape our unfinished business. If we think we can use the power to protect ourselves from getting hurt we are misinformed.
>
> On the other hand, if we open to the resources of the heart center we not only move through the crisis, we also enter a whole new place in life.

> And finally, what we want to discover is the current and destiny of our soul and then have the courage to live it so that we no longer need to defend or overly protect ourselves. When we come from our heart center, from a place of "not my will but Thine," we are brought to our soul's destiny.

My spiritual path has been a continuum of challenges—surrenders—and breakthroughs. Now, years later, I am still exploring life's many paradoxes.

Chapter 24

"Forgive, and be forgiven."
Mark 11:25.26

The "Heart Deepening" conference was followed immediately by "The Call of the Ancestors" Conference. Both were designed to move us deeper into our personal and collective unconscious—to appreciate good aspects but, more importantly, to see, acknowledge, and begin to heal other aspects as well. In this way we could begin to appreciate and honor—without judgment—all those who have come before us. These exercises would provide a rare opportunity for healing, forgiveness, and transformation.

Paraphrasing Brugh's opening statements: As a way to access our ancestral wisdom our approach will be through the techniques of meditation and sometimes dreams—and through the art of ritual. This work is to acknowledge that, on unconscious levels, these things exist and to honor in some way those resources made available to us, for whether this seems real to us or a little strange, the phenomena *IS*.

* * *

Brugh's understanding of dreams and how to interpret them, as well as his sensitivity to the energy field of the dreamer, was exceptional. He could comprehend dream imagery to reveal what was taking place in our deep psyche even when we, the dreamers, could not. In our first morning session, Brugh asked for dreams that might relate to us personally as well as to the larger collective. (Dreams sometimes, but not always, contain both.) The intention was to see what was presently unfolding, not just in one's personal life, but also on the world stage. A number of dreams were shared that revealed major shifts and changes occurring in both the personal and the collective unconscious, including mine.

> My dream:
> In the first sequence I feel a quickening of energy through my body (possibly from the energy that had been generated earlier that evening.)
> The next sequence—I am in a large living room in a small house. The room is crowded with people and we are watching television over each other's shoulders.
> In the next scene, I am in a theater with a large group of people watching the launching of a space mission. I am sitting behind Brugh and lean forward and say something to him, but don't remember what it was.
> Then, the dream changes and I am suddenly in this spaceship zooming out into space. Other symbols in the dream showed changes also taking place in the collective unconscious. A profound and prophetic dream!

Brugh's interpretation: At this stage of your life there seems to be an awakening of the vitality of something larger—something involved in the collective. The dream indicates a readiness to remove the masculine overlays you have used as a defense and begin to allow your feminine nature to emerge." His further comments: You have lived too small a life for who and what you are—somehow feeling you hadn't the resources to live the larger life. He saw as part of my illness, the fear of being humiliated or appearing unseemly. He also noted that I wear a mask in my voice to hide my feelings—meanwhile, underneath there is tremendous energy.

* * *

Along with the regular format of dream work and other spiritual exercises, this week we would also be making an ancestral mask from a mold of our faces. When decorated, the masks would reveal, on a deep level, a mystery surrounding our ancestral past. The masks would be part of our closing ceremony. After our first morning's dream session we gathered in the Lodge to begin. Creating the masks required a partner—who would apply a plaster of Paris mold to our face, and in turn, we would reciprocate. There was a palpable undercurrent of excitement and anticipation as we awaited instructions from Brugh and his assistants.

First, the room was cleared of furniture and plastic sheets were spread over the carpet. After choosing our partner, we claimed our floor space. Given shower caps and cotton strips to protect our hair we were ready. After a quick review of what was involved, we were taken—step by step—through the process. Strips of cheesecloth soaked in the plaster of Paris mix were first draped across the forehead, then across the nose, cheeks, chin, and neck. With each application air pockets were carefully smoothed out. The nostrils were left open, of course, but we could opt to have our mouth open or closed.

On the surface all went without a hitch. Underneath, however, there was some apprehension, at least on my part. There was the element of "Do I really trust this person (whom I only just met) to cover my face with this wet sticky stuff? "How will I breathe?" If others in the group had similar concerns, their fears and mine were assuaged under Brugh's guidance and expertise. Actually, the physical application and modeling of this gooey material wasn't as uncomfortable as I had imagined; nonetheless, I was glad when we were done.

Several days later our masks were dry and ready for painting and decorating. Long tables set up in the Lodge held an amazing array of items from which to choose. There were artist's paints and brushes, large boxes overflowing with scraps of luxurious fabrics, furs, intricate laces, ribbons, braids, and exotic feathers. Smaller boxes combined buttons, interesting stones, unique pieces of wood and metal, assorted bags of shiny glass beads, glittering sequins, and miscellaneous odds and ends. The experience felt a lot like rummaging through Grandma's attic.

Working within our group, we focused on our own mask. Brugh's only instruction was to quiet our conscious mind and let the unconscious forces come forward to orchestrate the creative process. Except for my prayer and meditation practice, I had little training in letting go and letting some other part of my psyche create without my conscious input. To put my conscious mind "on hold" and open to another part of my psyche was a big challenge for me. Every time I sat down with mask in hand, I had to reorient myself to this aim.

> Brugh's further comments about the immortality of unconscious patterns were very interesting:
> Although we as humans are a mortal process, the unconscious patterns we carry in our personal and clan lineage are immortal; meaning they have existed in human nature for eons and will continue to exist for eons. In some vital way, these immortal patterns, of light and dark forces, serve life. Whatever mask we wear as our outer persona—be it positive or negative—its opposite lies hidden in our interior. Again the paradox—we are both the light and the dark.

As I understood this—while our human life span is a mortal process, the mystical body is an immortal process, carrying our DNA patterns, both positive and negative, down through the ages. I did wonder in what way one's negative patterns serve life. Are they meant to plague us until such time as we awaken to a new possibility?

My impression, as a child and now as an adult, was that the adults in my family were by-and-large honest, upright citizens, diligent and hardworking, kind and generous, and strong in their religious faith. I believe I inherited some of these fine qualities. However, realizing that every family has their share of both the good and bad in human nature, I also realized that my family, including myself, was no exception. Contemplating all that I was proud of in my family and in myself, I also found some things I wished were different.

Understanding that we can't have the light without its shadow—was a deepening realization. Working with dreams and images, and from hi-intensity exercises, revealed this inner world of light and shadow, allowing me to see some of these ancestral patterns. Working also with the heart centering meditation, I held a place of unconditional love and compassion for all of my ancestors.

* * *

Until now I had not considered the dimensions and complexities of my heritage, nor what it meant that my DNA contained the past, present, and future history of my lineage. Suddenly I realized a larger reality—that I did not stand alone or apart from these influences. As Brugh said, "each family member is given their own unique and individual slice of the family pie." I pondered what attributes of good and bad were in my slice.

From Brugh's many years of conference work with students and their dreams, he discovered that these unconscious patterns, constructive *and* destructive, control our behavior. The message was twofold: to heal a destructive family pattern it must first be brought to consciousness and recognized for what it is, either through dreams or other divining modalities. Only then—from our heart center—that place of total love, acceptance, and forgiveness—can healing begin.

* * *

Mentioned in earlier chapters, the pattern of **fear** has continued to inform me of its presence over the years, through some powerful dreams as well as in the challenge of writing my story. The recurring dream of a dark figure following me* and my ancestral dream** seem to indicate that fear has haunted me and my family for a very long time. Something very dark indeed must be buried in the collective psyche of my clan, and in my genes, to have manifested such a profound ancestral image.

Also, fears of expressing my thoughts, feelings, and opinions have always been held in check by a strong need to conform to society's beliefs and standards. Indeed, taking a stand against the status quo, whether in private or in public, was simply unacceptable. At the same time, though I sometimes felt resentful, I never defied parental rules; nor did I question aloud the established rules of Southern society or the dogma of my Southern Baptist religion. Besides, I had no better substitute at the time.

I probably felt inadequate to defend my position; yet at a deeper level, it may have also been an unconscious pattern reminding me

* Chapter 7

** Chapter 13

"not to disturb this state of clan-imposed harmony. Later, as a student and teacher of Religious Science, I began to see how unexpressed thoughts and feelings adversely affect one's state of health. I had learned the hard way that when life's troublesome issues go unresolved and unexpressed the soul will initiate a crisis of some kind to bring us back into harmony and balance.

We were well into decorating our masks when Brugh stated that none of us are in charge of what these masks will be when completed. "As the masks come forward—they are not there to enhance our ego—rather they are there in a very deep way." As my mask neared completion I could not have been more amazed to see it take on the character of an Egyptian noblewoman, or Priestess.

Staring at me was a face painted and bejeweled, wearing an Egyptian-style headdress, richly decorated with peacock feathers. Even though Brugh had told us the masks did not reflect us from a personal level but rather a transcendent level, I still had to wonder what immortal pattern was being presented in a mask of such antiquity. Suddenly, I was thrown centuries, rather than generations, back in time. Grasping such a distant past seemed quite beyond me.

Brugh asked "that we make ourselves fully vulnerable to the patterns of transformation that are unique to who and what we are and to our next staging, whatever that may be." He said, "Open to the mystery of the collective—to your roots—to the depths of your soul....then call upon the wisdom of your ancestors for the courage to live what is out there for you. Our closing will be the coalescence of all of these forces."

Again, we were reminded that we would be invoking forces more powerful than our personalities and, therefore, it was vital that our heart center be open. Part of our initiation will be to deliver up the currant of the mask and what we stand for—and then let that force speak through us."

* * *

As in all our closing ceremonies, sacred music and a profusion of beautiful flowers created the perfect ambience. Wearing ritual garments of white, carrying our mask and a spray of flowers, we entered single file to form our circle. When all were seated we were reminded to see our circle as sacred and immortal—as part of a vast mystical body. Then, deepening within ourselves, allowing ourselves to be clear channels through which our ancestors could speak, we entered into a silent heart-centering meditation.

In this silence we waited for what seemed a very long time before anyone spoke. Between long silences, waiting for an inner prompting, one by one, we began. At one point I heard my voice say, "Stand on our shoulders." Later, whether it was the same voice or another that came through, I don't know, but the message was more an appreciation of our seeking their wisdom.

These are the words as I recall them: "Those of my clan welcome each and every one of the clans' representatives here. Our wisdom to you would be to realize, acknowledge, and call forth the resources of your ancestors for strength, for healing, for support, for courage, for whatever it is you need to stand tall, speak your word, and ask from your heart center." As each one spoke the heightened wisdom of their ancestors, our heartfelt response was a collective "Amen." Brugh gave a final tribute to those who had come to share with us. The following day, with mask in tow, I returned home deeply moved by having been a part of this miraculous and mystifying evening with the ancestors.

* * *

Thoughts of my ancestors kept returning the following week. Carefully unwrapping the family *Bible* inherited from my maternal great-grandparent's, dating back to 1849, its pages crisp and fragile, I hoped to find personal letters or notes I might have previously overlooked, yet there was nothing more than statistics of births, marriages, and deaths. Actually the genealogical records kept by both sides of my family revealed little of the character of my ancestors and nothing of the hardships and challenges they faced. Perhaps personal stories, letters, and written documents have been kept, treasured, and tucked away by some distant cousins. But for all those I have known, there is little more than a few letters, lots of old photographs, and some childhood memories.

When I closed my eyes to think on these things a picture of my maternal grandfather and great-grandfather came to mind. From what little I knew of them, their lives seemed in stark contrast—a dramatic example of the pairs of opposites within our clan. As a young teen, visiting my grandparent's, I found my grandfather an enigma—a silent and somber presence. Naturally, I was afraid of him.

By contrast, his father, my great-grandfather, made a positive impact on me when, in his nineties, he spent three months with our family in Mississippi. (I knew he had been a successful farmer in Georgia—but in those days, the resources of vacation time and money to visit family living so far away was not an option.) Thirteen years old at the time, I was impressed not only by his keen intelligence, friendly and gracious manner, but also by his physical, mental, and spiritual vitality.

In my mind's eye, I can see him sitting under a tree in an adjacent pasture on a warm sunny autumn day reading his *Bible*—with Bessie, our Jersey heifer, grazing nearby. I had a distinct feeling then, and even more so now, that he was a wise old soul. I feel our family has been blessed, perhaps beyond our imagining, by his presence, his prayers, and his spiritual wisdom.

Nonetheless, other questions began to arise—"What was his relationship with his son, my grandfather?" From my perspective, they seemed so different. I wondered if they might have been estranged. If so, what could have been their unresolved issues? Indeed, might there have been an issue between my mother and my grandfather? Recalling now signs I had previously overlooked—that I never heard my mother speak of him, nor did he ever, in my memory, visit in our home. Now, considering the long-standing conflict between my sister and me, what ancestral patterns do we carry that keep us from coming together as a loving family?

Would we ever understand the origin of our ideological split and allow it to be reconciled. I was beginning to believe, through my heart-centering work with Brugh, this was possible. I feel there is no one to blame for the past—not my ancestors, my sister, nor myself. Everyone in my life was (and is) there for a reason—each one has contributed to my life experience in some valuable way—teaching me about life and about myself.

I am indeed grateful for this opportunity to express my love and appreciation for all who have been a part of my life. To those I have misjudged and those who have misjudged me—feeling love and forgiveness toward each one—I ask forgiveness. Acknowledging the sacrifices my parents made for my sisters and me, I am so appreciative of their love and desire to give us a life better than theirs, for their faith and belief in God, and for the inner strength and character that fortified and sustained them through Judy's long illness. I ask a blessing for us all.

Chapter 25

"And ye shall know the truth, and the truth shall set you free."
John 8:32

After my last conference with Dr. Joy in 1992, I attended a number of weekend workshops to stay current with his work. However, when my hearing became a problem I knew I must stay at home with what I had learned. I remembered him asking someone who kept coming back to his conferences, "Why are you still here? Why aren't you out there doing what you do?" At this stage of my life I had to ask the same question. Why wasn't I writing the book I had begun in the mid 1980's?

Brugh once said to me, "You will either live your life or you will write about it." I believe he meant I could choose to live my life expressing greater joy and passion in the present moment, or I could write of past events and circumstances that have brought me thus far. The message I seemed to be getting, however, was to follow both leanings—to live *and* write with greater joy and passion. When the idea of writing first presented itself, aware that my epiphany experience had been unbelievable in the telling, I wondered if a written version would be believed. Part of me was intrigued with the idea of sharing this incredible story, but another part was decidedly reluctant. After all, I had few writing skills; nonetheless, there was this strong urge to begin.

During these intervening years, many conscious and unconscious "what if's" came forward, creating more writing blocks. I knew the course my life had taken would be seen as a contradiction of traditional beliefs. I also knew that people were quite naturally fearful and defensive when their beliefs were threatened. (Some I know feel that questioning their beliefs is questioning the existence of God.) I understood that people, comfortable with their religious life, would prefer not to disturb their beliefs in the light of new material. I believed that this was also the attitude of clergy and lay leaders as well. After all, church leaders had more to lose if they felt their beliefs were endangered.

Based on my unhappy encounters with a few fundamentalists, and on literature I had read over the years regarding some of their beliefs, I expected my book to meet some hostility. Still, I felt that a "Power Greater than I" was coaxing me to stand up and speak my truth, even if some might not understand—even if some might oppose me. In the past, by avoiding confrontations in my outer life I fought many inner battles over such cowardice. Yet, in spite of real and imagined fears, the inner strength and courage to keep writing has truly amazed me. With each small success, rich insights and revelations came—until the next challenge.

* * *

In my younger days I could not reconcile the judgmental God of the *Old Testament* with the Loving God of the *New Testament;* or determine which of the two Creation stories was true. How could God be both judgmental and loving? Could I be a beloved child of God and also a lowly sinner? Now I realize that these truths are paradoxical—that God is a God of Law as well as a God of Love—and that we are both the beloved *and* the sinner. Amazingly, we are a paradox of both human and divine; simultaneously spiritual beings created, perfect, and complete in the mind and heart of God—for a time living on this earthly plane in an imperfect and incomplete state.

Identifying who we are with our visible, physical, material world and our five physical senses, we have forgotten, if we ever knew, that we also live and move and have our being in Spirit. This profound truth—that God, as a Living Spirit, indwells us—is quite beyond the reach of most Western minds; and as such, remains virtually lost to us. Left with feelings of separation from our spiritual roots, and burdened with real or imagined guilt, we live in ignorance of the nearness of Spirit. In my opinion, our religious institutions have failed us yet again.

* * *

Paradoxes are to be found everywhere and in everything throughout nature. There are, indeed, two sides to everything.

> In his Essay on Compensation, Ralph Waldo Emerson explains "polarity as action and reaction in every part of nature; in darkness and light; in heat and cold; in the ebb and flow of waters; in male and female; in the inspiration and expiration of plants and animals; in the systole and diastole of the heart; in the undulations of fluids and of sound…." Indeed, we cannot have one without the other, each half makes a whole.

Life's paradoxes are to be found throughout the *Holy Bible,* and even though they were such an early mystery to me, the *Bible* has been the solid foundation on which I have ultimately built my faith. Other teachings later explained and clarified these paradoxical truths. When Jesus said, "Be in this world, but not of it," he was asking his disciples to hold in consciousness a higher Truth of God, Everywhere-Present, in the midst of all human affairs—especially in our darkest hour. We are likewise challenged to do the same, that we might be lifted above the fray—to declare peace in the midst of chaos, love in the midst of hate, health in the midst of disease, plenty in the midst of poverty, joy in the midst of sorrow.

* * *

My personal paradox is that while my outer life from birth was a positive experience, my inner life was a trunk full of fears and feelings of inadequacy. Blessed early on with a loving extended family and good friends, good health for the first half of my life, and a wonderful husband and children, my first glimpse into my inner world occurred in the late 1950's in a small encounter group at our Methodist Church in Tulsa, Oklahoma. Our assistant minister had asked us to tell the group something that we liked about ourselves. My first reaction was acute embarrassment to even think of something I liked about myself and then actually share that with others!

Then I turned to a lovely young lady on my left who, with obvious joy, unabashedly stated that she liked herself because she was a child of God. With sudden clarity I saw that my self-image was not that of a child of God, but of a sinner. I believe this sinner image, implanted at an early age, had engendered feelings of self-loathing, and left me unable to love myself as God loves me. As children born of God we are also products of our ancestral lineage, our religious indoctrination, formal education, community environment, and personal experiences—for better or worse. Because of these many influences, we grow up perceiving ourselves as "either/or"—either a God creation or a sinner —not realizing the paradox that we are both.

* * *

Above all other commandments, LOVE is the COMMANDMENT we are meant to obey. Loving God has been easy, loving my neighbor has sometimes been hard, loving my enemies harder still, and hardest of all, has been loving and forgiving my little human self for all its mistakes and weaknesses. The task of upgrading my self image from "lowly sinner" to that of "the beloved" has been a lengthy process. Understanding the necessity of accepting and appreciating *all* aspects of who and what I am, not just those parts I like, I now embrace from my heart center those traits that seem "antithetical to the self, and begin to love them into health and wholeness."

* * *

Walking the labyrinth of my spiritual path has been quite an adventure—and the adventure continues. I am reminded of a series of seven woodcuts Dr. Joy saw in India that depicts the seeker's journey. The first one is of a monk standing in a marketplace. The next five woodcuts show him traveling through populated towns and small villages, trudging alone over hill and dale, along quiet country lanes, traversing mountains, and fording streams: in effect, encountering all aspects of nature and human life. Another woodcut added later shows the monk back in the marketplace. The marketplace is the same but he, himself, is profoundly changed. He now sees everything with different eyes.

This is a beautiful metaphor for my personal journey. While my physical environment has changed somewhat, the major changes have been within. How I once perceived myself in relationship to life—and how very differently I perceive myself now in all of my relationships is nothing short of miraculous. Now, having established a connection to Spirit through my heart center, I see with different eyes a whole new world.

* * *

It has taken many years to make this journey—from feeling so separated from God, my Life, to a deep knowing that God is a Spirit, ever with us, in us, over and beyond us—in all of life. I have no doubt that God wants for each of us our highest and greatest good; yet according to the law of God, we can only have what we *believe* we can have, what we *believe* we can do, and what we *believe* we can be. These divine gifts come only from *our asking, believing, and trusting* in such a profound truth. A belief in this higher truth, and in ourselves as God's creation, can *quite literally* lift us out of our limited beliefs into new possibilities and opportunities.

I believe all peoples of the world are created from the same Cosmic Light/Energy, given sovereignty over our individual soul, as well as inner resources beyond our conscious awareness. Knowing this, we would be wise to seek first our own inner wisdom for what is right and good and true, rather than relying too heavily on other people's beliefs and opinions. To know the truth and be set free in that truth is not only a privilege, and a birthright, but our sole responsibility. Teachers and scriptures can lead us to truth but, ultimately, it is up to us as individuals to learn the truth for ourselves.

Chapter 26

"Wisdom is the principal thing; therefore, get wisdom:
And with all thy getting, get understanding."
Proverbs 4:7

Since the beginning of time, humanity has sought after wisdom greater than their human understanding, which suggests an inherent longing in the human heart to reconnect with God, our Source. In my personal quest for wisdom and spiritual understanding over the last thirty-seven years, I found many truths throughout the *Holy Bible*, in the Science of Mind teachings and in Mystery School. Eastern and Western traditions were explored, as well as a wide range of metaphysical, philosophical, and psychological subjects. Finding a measure of truth in each that satisfied my soul, I realized none contradicted my core belief in God as the Creator of life, nor undermined my belief in the power and significance of Jesus' life and teachings.

From the *Old Testament* of the *Christian Bible*, my first introduction to God was as Father. The emphasis in the *New Testament* was on Christ Jesus as the Son of God. In *The Science of Mind*, the perspective shifted to God as Divine Mind, and Jesus as fully conscious of his oneness with God, the Father. From the Hindu mystics, the emphasis was on God as Divine Mother. In Buddhism, the point was to live in joy and appreciation of "the Eternal Now." From Mystery School, the focus was awakening, through dreams and spiritual exercises, to the God/Goddess; the Christ/Buddha; the Masculine/Feminine principle at work in us, through us, and over us. The development of the heart center provides a safe passage into our shadow material for healing and transformation.

I now believe that no one faith or tradition has a monopoly on God's Truth. Rather, I believe Truth has been scattered indiscriminately by our Creator throughout human history, among all peoples of all nations and cultures. In the 1970's I found a book, published in 1946, by Lewis Browne, titled *The World's Great Scriptures, An anthology of the sacred books of the ten principal religions*. Here the emphasis was on the similarities rather than the differences in religions.

> In the Preface he says,
> There is an increasing wonder nowadays about religions other than our own, and that is a good thing. …Wonder is imperative if we are to begin fitting ourselves for this world we live in. Bigotry was endurable in earlier times, for the planet was roomier then, and peoples could keep somewhat apart. But today our world is so shrunken that bigotry has become like cholera in a crowded camp. Our first need, therefore, is sanitation. Our minds must be opened up, swept clean, thoroughly aired.…Wonder must give way to questioning, uncertainty to research.…To know what our neighbors believe we must go to their scriptures.…
> There are three aspects to every great religion: faith, hope, and charity. Faith is the theology, hope is the ritual, and charity is the ethics.….In one form or another, the Golden Rule is found in the scriptures of *all* the major religions.

As a New Age Christian, I have added to my beliefs in God and Jesus, the Buddhist discipline of meditation as a way to quiet my mind, calm my emotions, and relax my body, as well as the concept of "mindfulness,"—appreciating life moment to moment.

> Paramahansa Yogananda writes in his book, <u>Man's Eternal Quest:</u>
> To meditate truly is the highest form of activity that man can perform, and it is the most balanced way to find God. If you work all the time you may become mechanical and lose Him in preoccupation with your duties, and if you

seek Him only through discriminative thought you may lose Him in the labyrinths of endless reasoning, and if you cultivate only devotion for God, your development may become merely emotional. But meditation combines and balances all these approaches.

In the 1980's, while serving as a practitioner in the Seattle Church of Religious Science, I took a six-week workshop from Ron Zieler, a young man who had lived for five years in Tibet as a Buddhist monk. He introduced us to the concept of "Mindfulness"—which meant bringing one's attention to life as it is happening in every present moment. In reality, life unfolds as a succession of "eternal now" moments—each meant to be appreciated for what it offers. It came as quite a shock to realize that, for much of my life, the present moment had been lost by my focus on past or projected future events.

One evening Ron invited a Buddhist monk to chant for us. In the beginning the sounds seemed harsh and guttural, the words foreign and unintelligible, with a monotonous sing-song rhythm, yet at one point a subtle but definite shift occurred. My constantly busy mind "unhooked" briefly—allowing me to enter a deeper silence, to listen for that inner voice. Another special gift from Ron was a simple refrain played on a small keyboard of Eastern origin. This tune has stayed with me as a gentle reassurance of God's Ever-Present Love.

Each line is repeated and sung as a prayer.

Dr. Rodney Romney, now a retired American Baptist minister, in his book, *Journey to Inner Space, Finding God-in-us,* writes in his chapter, "Let There Be Light:"

> The Creation Story, recorded in Genesis, tells in the opening verse that God created light before he created the sun and the earth. God first made light as spiritual energy and from that light created all things. We, therefore, are not made of solid, impenetrable matter (*which scientists have proven*)—instead, we are made of light energy. This primal energy is what we call God.
>
> When the *Bible* says we are made in God's image, it means we are constructed of the very energy force which is God, and while this light is projected from etheric realms beyond the earth, it is also at the center of every person's being.

I had never heard God expressed before as Energy by a man of the cloth. "Spirit," yes—but not the term "Energy," yet this is what I had felt in my own experience.

* * *

In May 1995, I attended a Spiritualist Conference in Montreal, Canada at the urging of my friend, Carol Varley. Although I had gained as much as I could from my conferences with Dr. Joy, I still could not interpret dreams at pattern level—an ability Brugh felt was primary. I thought perhaps exposure to people advanced in extrasensory perception might help. Many presenters from around the globe came to share their unique spiritual gifts. One presenter I delighted in was Divaldo Franco, introduced as Brazil's foremost "Spiritist."

Through his interpreter, Divaldo began by saying that he had more dead friends than live ones. It seems that when people died in his village and surrounding countryside their spirit would often appear to him to intercede on their behalf, asking forgiveness from certain individuals they had wronged. His ability to communicate with deceased spirits was evident at a very young age, and was a natural part of his life. A host of interesting speakers covered a wide spectrum of related subjects. In addition, a large group of interfaith leaders from the world's great religions, including the Native American traditions, gathered in a closing ceremony to affirm "A New Heaven and a New Earth."

Nonetheless, this conference was for psychics, mediums, and others naturally attuned to psycho-spiritual realms. As I didn't fit these descriptions, I felt very much an "outsider looking in" the entire week—unable to connect with what these people were experiencing. Aware of elements of truth being presented, I believed these people were authentic in what they were sharing. Again, I found nothing to contradict my core beliefs. Overall, my exposure to these "psycho-spiritually adept" souls was a good thing—in the sense that they offered me yet another glimpse into "the many mansions in my Father's house." (Taken from *John 14:2)*

* * *

I appreciated this quote by Gregory of Nyssa, in his Commentary on the Canticles, as it sums up my belief that truth is scattered at home and abroad.

> He says, "....we ought not to despise any teaching of piety, but, as we fly over the meadow of the inspired doctrines, we ought to gather from each one something for our store of wisdom."

From many avenues I have learned what I vitally needed to learn—about life, about God, and about myself—enough to bring a deep sense of joy and contentment to my soul. Daily prayers and affirmations have been essential to train my thoughts and beliefs in a new direction, and steady me in this endeavor. Asking for what I needed in any given moment (not in worldly goods but in spiritual tender) has become a daily practice, as has quiet listening for inner guidance.

Occasionally a Bible verse will pop into my mind as just what I need to hear. One example is this jewel—where Jesus said, "My yoke is easy and my burden is light."*(Matt. 11:30)* Indeed, when I can relax and let go in surrender to the Divine Will, my burdens *are* lifted! It took me awhile to learn that too much effort actually impedes the activity of Spirit. Indeed, trusting Spirit to work on the invisible plane without my help other than to pray, listen, and wait, has taken a *long* time. Knowledge and understanding has come incrementally—over time and in degrees. Not all knowledge and understanding—only that which I was prepared and ready to receive.

* * *

Viewing my life now in my understanding and sense of God as an Ever-Present Spirit—and where I was in the beginning in my sense of a God so distant as to seem unreal—I am truly in awe of the power of Spirit to lead me out of the wilderness of my ignorance and unbelief. The driving force in my search for truth has been this overriding hunger and thirst for wisdom and understanding. Finding the courage to move, one step at a time, through my fears, meeting my shadow at every turn, has revealed inner resources I didn't know I had.

Now I am in total awe of such a profound mystery as the God of Creation—the Giver of my life, of all life, and all blessings. Far too complex to fathom from my three-dimensional perch, thoughts of God as Infinite Spirit—an Invisible Essence, Everywhere Present, throughout time and space, and beyond—deepens the mystery. Remembering that God is Love, and Divine Love is the *only* Power that can overcome hate and fear in me and in the world, I continue to dwell on the divine attributes of my heart center. Indeed, hate and fear cannot reside in a heart centered and grounded in unconditional love, deep compassion, innate harmony, and a real sense of a Holy Presence.

* * *

According to Revelations, we are now experiencing the end of the world as we have known it, and the beginning of a new millennium. Alongside the crumbling of the old order, of what no longer works for the greater good, there is a quickening within of the Holy Spirit, reminding us of our spiritual roots, telling us we are the beloved—that we always were, and always will be. The pivotal message of Jesus was to teach us the transforming power of this All-embracing, All-inclusive Love. I believe Jesus was pointing the way to the third aspect of The Trinity—the Holy Spirit—when he made the statement, "The Kingdom of Heaven is not lo, here or lo, there, but within."

* * *

On my journey there have been leaps in consciousness—from fear and ignorance to a small measure of understanding and a profound faith in the existence and love of God. As finite beings, we cannot know the Infinite, yet, there is much Spirit would have us know of the Love that enfolds us, the power for good inherent within us, and the wisdom of our Inner Counsel to guide us through the darkness into the Light. So now I say—what if religion and the scientific world of reason scoff—no longer will I keep hidden in my heart this glorious secret. I am impelled to speak it and write of it—for better or worse. In my personal and intimate experience of God I put my trust. The last verse of a poem I wrote many years ago says it best.

Now—my heart no longer
A place for tears of sadness,
No longer cold and dark,
For the spark of light that I am
Found the Source of all Light,
The Great I AM,
And I am no more sorely troubled.

Epilogue

A PRAYER

May the gradual understanding

Of our oneness as a human family

Bring peace out of chaos;

Wisdom out of ignorance;

And in all human relations,

May that which is hidden and dishonest

Be revealed and healed—

Not only in our nation and our world,

But in ourselves as well.

Appendix A

(Credentials and brief biography of Dr. Brugh Joy, from his book, *Joy's Way*).

Dr. Joy's credentials are impressive. His Pre-Med education was from the University of Southern California. A member of the Phi Beta Kappa Scholastic Society, he graduated Magna cum laude in 1960. He completed his education at U.S.C. (1960-64) where he was a member of Alpha Omega Alpha Honorary Medical Scholastic Society. His internship and last year of Internal Medicine was spent at John Hopkins Hospital in Baltimore, Maryland from 1964 to 1966. He then completed his Internal Medicine residency at the Mayo Clinic in Rochester, Minnesota in 1968. Entering the Navy, he was stationed at Balboa Naval Hospital in San Diego from 1968 to 1970. Board Certified in Internal Medicine in June of 1970, he began a private practice in Los Angeles that same year, specializing in diseases of the heart and lungs.

While practicing orthodox medicine, he met a most unusual teacher of meditation and expanded states of consciousness. Her name was Eunice Hurt. A meeting with Eunice in late 1971, her death in November 1972, and some of the things she taught him are covered in his book, Joy's Way. It was through this teacher that he was able to entertain alternatives to the healing process.

Subsequent events led to his discovery of human body energy fields and his capacity to influence the patient by affecting these fields with the hand, either in a light touch, or at a distance from the patient's body. He found he could specifically induce a heightened state of well-being and healing potential in his patients. This discovery occurred one day in early 1973 while he was performing a routine physical exam on a young healthy male. For no apparent reason a strange thought entered his awareness. He wondered if he could feel any energy radiating from this person. Much to his surprise he felt a warm cloud over the upper mid-abdomen radiating three or four inches in a cylinder-like shape from the body surface. Nothing in his training could account for this phenomenon and over the next three months he mapped these radiating fields from the head, neck, chest, abdomen and extremities of various patients. He had no idea at the time of their significance or their patterning. He called the technique of passing his hand back and forth, palm down, six to eight inches above the patient's body "scanning."

Browsing through the Bodhi Tree Bookstore in Los Angeles soon afterward, he came across a book open to an ancient drawing of a man seated in meditation with circles and strange inscriptions drawn on his body. They were in the exact location of the places he had found the energy fields radiating over his patient's bodies the previous three months. He was not so much ecstatic over finding that these energy fields had been known as chakras for thousands of years in Eastern religions and culture as he was relieved and happy that his findings were confirmed. Having intuitively discovered these energy fields in the human body, using them as an effective diagnostic tool in his medical practice, he wanted to learn more about them.

Having distinguished himself as a medical doctor, he abruptly left his practice, following a life-threatening illness in 1974, and travelled to Findhorn, Scotland and to Egypt, India, and Nepal to observe and study these energy systems. On his return he opened a conference center in California, and later in Arizona, for people interested in learning about body energy and its healing power.

In his early conference work, he taught health professionals and others how to heal through a very caring nurturing touch. What he found was, although this kind of touch influenced and aided an individual to heal, there were certain leaps in consciousness, way beyond caring and nurturing that could lead to "transformation, renovation and new possibility." He called these "sacred states of consciousness." He began to develop some techniques, first of all, to prepare people to enter these sacred places of the psyche, and then to utilize and channel these energies within themselves, and later, to share with others. Such an undertaking needed the help of a transcendent energy. This resulted in the development of the heart center as a safe passage into one's shadow material.

* * *

Dr. Joy's training in the 70's was to see disease as an error and doctors as the "white knights." Many physicians customarily treated their patients as though they were not capable of making decisions concerning their health. Brugh's feeling was that the majority of patients weren't ready to take on the discipline, the focus, and the insights that come forward when one begins to realize what the unconscious elements of disease are.

Gradually, Brugh began to see that disease was something that served an individual; that it was not, in itself, a victim process but played a role in the development of that individual. He confessed that as he began to look at disease from this perspective, he saw things he had never seen before. For one thing, he saw that one could self-heal and self-nourish oneself; but to do so required a lot of self-honesty. At this writing Dr Joy continues his conference work.

Books:
Joy's Way, published in 1974 by J. P. Tarcher, Inc.
9110 Sunset Blvd., Los Angeles, Ca. 90069
Avalanche, published in 1990 by Ballantine Books,
a division of Random House, Inc., New York

C.D.'s and tapes:
The Spiral Meditation
Temple by the Sea
The Realization of Presence

For Conference information contact bjikaren@aol.com

CPSIA information can be obtained at www.ICGtesting.com
Printed in the USA
LVOW11s1440240914

405661LV00001BA/15/P

9 781608 440030